WHY HILLARY LOST

ROLAND MEDIA DISTRIBUTION

WHY HILLARY LOST

ARVIN VOHRA

Published and distributed by
Roland Media Distribution
www.RMDGlobal.net

Library of Congress Control Number: 2016961749
ISBN: 978-0-9801446-7-3

CONTENTS

INTRODUCTION

Donald Trump's upset victory over Hillary Clinton has left many Americans shocked, enraged, disturbed, and afraid. The political polls and pundits were completely wrong. Common sense was wrong.

On the surface, Trump had literally everything going against him. His own party leaders had rejected him, and withdrawn their endorsements and support. All of America heard him bragging about his aggressive approach to women. He had been accused of sexual assault by over a dozen women.

The Republican governor of the vital swing state of Ohio publicly wrote in John McCain instead of voting for Trump. In fact, that same governor, John Kasich, even ran ads against Trump. (Trump later won Ohio.)

Trump had made one political blunder after another. He had mocked a disabled reporter, insulted Muslims, veterans, and anyone else he could find. Despite being a billionaire, he had not paid income taxes. His university was under investigation. He had never held public office. Actors, writers, and comedians were openly opposing him.

On the other hand, Clinton had relatively few problems. There was an issue involving classified emails that, frankly, around zero percent of the population understood. There was a Whitewater real estate scandal from a few decades ago that no one seemed to have any interest in.

Clinton was endorsed by more newspapers and more celebrities. She had much more positive media attention. She had decades of political experience. Most people believed she had won both debates against Trump.

The odds of his winning were ranked at around 15%. Experts predicted that Clinton would win in a massive electoral landslide.

Now that the politically unthinkable has happened, many Democratic voters are struggling to make sense of the results. From their perspectives, it seems that:

1. A huge percentage of the American population is racist, xenophobic, and homophobic.
2. Americans, including millions of women, hate powerful women.
3. People really, really care a lot about email servers.

This book is designed to examine those possible explanations and others, in order to give political groups the information they need to address the issues this election has brought to light.

A LITTLE ABOUT ME

My own unusual background, as a half political insider, half
political outsider, gives me a perspective that, if nothing
else, is different. I am the Vice Chair of a now small, but
rapidly growing, political party called the Libertarian Party.

In my political work, I have traveled around the
country, and met people of all political backgrounds and walks
of life. I have recruited and/or trained dozens of candidates and
hundreds of activists. I prefer to work on the ground, getting
the real story from people in various locations.

I also am heavily involved in the social media
strategy of the Libertarian Party, which has one of
the most dynamic and forward thinking social media
presences in American politics, despite our comparatively
small size and budget. Part of that work is learning to
keep the pulse of different political groups and factions,
using both personal and mathematical measurements. I
grew up inside the Beltway, and I have been surrounded by
politicians, government contractors, and federal employees
for my entire life. I grew up with the kids of the big evil
lobbyists. I have been versed in Washington culture since
elementary school, including the vital nuances of political
strategy often ignored by the press.

Both of my parents were civil servants – my father
worked for the Department of Energy, and my mother
for the state Health Department. Later, they both became

entrepreneurs. I am also an entrepreneur, and understand the mindset and goals of small businesses.

I am an ethnic minority, and have seen life from that perspective. I have been made fun of for my ethnicity, and even been discriminated against. Even though I am not Muslim, I look Arab (my parents are actually Indian), and I have received plenty of discrimination because of that. (It can take me a while to get through airport security, to say the least.)

Politically, I had no preference between Clinton and Trump. My goal was to have the Libertarian candidate, Gary Johnson, break previous Libertarian records (which he ended up shattering). I'm one of the few national level political strategists who can be objectively neutral about the results.

From this disinterested, half-insider, half-outsider perspective, I hope to help people understand why Clinton lost. I do not pretend to know all the details or have all the answers. Anyone who says that is either lying or delusional. But I believe this analysis will help Democrats, Republicans, Libertarians, Greens, Constitutionalists, and Independents understand the 2016 election.

During the next months and years, there will be dozens of books written on this topic that will examine every single technical angle of this election. They will look at percentage turnouts, the dollars spent on media buys, and the numerical data that political analysts love. But despite my own background as a former actuary, I do not think this election was primarily about that.

This book will focus on the psychological, emotional, and cultural forces that shaped the election.

One final note: I call this book *Why Hillary Lost*, not *Why Trump Won*, because I believe that the strategic mistakes made by the Clinton campaign, the Democratic Party, and the progressive movement allowed the Trump victory. Trump got about 1.5 million more votes than McCain had in 2008. Clinton got over 6 million votes fewer than Obama had in 2008. She somehow lost millions of the voters Obama had brought to the Democratic Party. Had she kept even half of those voters, she would have been elected.

The 2016 election was a race to the bottom, and Hillary Clinton won.

THE DEMOCRATIC ECHO CHAMBER

OUTREACH

Politics depends on outreach. The massive success of the Democratic Party over the last 8 years has been a clear testament to that fact.

The outreach that has taken the form of traditional advertising, social media, and, most importantly, face-to-face discussions. The personal conversations, not between politicians and constituents, but between friends and family members, was effectively used to influence the elections of 2008 and 2012. Young Democrats with strong talking points were winning over both shy Democrats and independents. The debates on campuses, in classrooms, and in personal conversations allowed Democrats to spread their message and gain votes.

The Democratic National Committee obviously knows the importance of this. They are great at arming their supporters with arguments on various issues. For example, through its creation of the ingenious website "YourRepublicanUncle.com", the DNC helped provide people with debate ammunition to win family arguments at Thanksgiving. And people were winning many of those arguments with that ammunition and other Democratic rhetoric.

But in the past few years, the brilliantly effective Democratic strategy of turning each activist into an effective outreach debater has shifted. This has not been done by the DNC. It has been a cultural shift taking place in colleges and other intellectual centers, and it is known as the Safe Space movement.

SAFE SPACES HURT DEMOCRATIC OUTREACH

The safe space movement began as a way to allow LGBT people to communicate in a safe environment that allowed them to discuss their experience of marginalization without fear of being attacked. This idea is not new. Every support group in the world operates from a similar principle. When you speak at an Alcoholics Anonymous or Narcotics Anonymous meeting, you know that you will be supported, not attacked (even if you admit to something embarrassing, self-destructive, or illegal). Just as in an AA meeting, hate speech is not tolerated in a safe space, and encouragement, sympathy, and support abound.

But there's a huge difference: size.

Alcoholics Anonymous meetings happen at clearly defined locations to which one can go. Inside of an AA meeting, a person knows that there will be no judgements, only encouragement and understanding. But AA has never tried to convert other locations into safe spaces; they do not spread beyond the walls of the room. People who attend AA meetings understand that the general public outside of an AA meeting is unlikely to applaud them for being sober for 12 hours, nor is the public likely to be as supportive of prior miscreant behavior while under the influence.

The creation of small sanctuaries for people to use as needed has seen great success; a small sanctuary makes people feel safe. The safe space movements on campuses and in other spaces, however, have received some backlash and a whole lot of resentment. Why? Because safe spaces attempt to turn huge areas into sanctuaries. That ends up limiting intellectual freedoms. Students lose their freedom to attend potentially exciting or enlightening (or controversial) invited speaker events. They lose their freedom to engage in passionate and intellectual (and possibly upsetting) debate. They feel they can no longer freely explore intellectual questions.

The average college student does not want to create malicious groups to harass other students. The average college student wants to learn, discover, challenge pre-existing ideas and build new ones. All of that requires freedom, and safe spaces have denied students that freedom.

Even college faculty and administration are opposing the safe space movement. For example, this year the University of Chicago wrote a letter to incoming freshmen advising them of the university's "commitment to freedom of inquiry and expression". As a result of this commitment, the letter explains that "trigger warnings" and "safe spaces" are specifically not condoned.

Furthermore, while the idea of having greater and greater sections of cities marked off as safe spaces may seem to strengthen the Democratic position, it actually weakens its position in the battle of ideas. From a strategic perspective, safe spaces are functionally blackout zones in which progressives cannot convert anyone. Since no one can voice opposition, no one can have his views changed.

Safe spaces are not designed to be places of debate or persuasion. Instead of trying to win intellectual debates, the safe space method uses social pressure. If you are not supportive of everything within the safe space, then you're kicked out, screamed at, or silenced. This alienates everyone on any side other than the Democratic side (and has even alienated some Democrats).

For example, suppose a white student decides to wear blackface as part of a costume. Intellectual debate might involve asking why it is important to him, or explaining why doing so is disrespectful or just in poor taste. It can even involve spirited or angry disagreement.

But by the end, that white student might be convinced that the costume was not such a good idea.

The safe space approach has involved such responses as: demanding that he stop, using abusive language, threats, and graffiti, or even creating enough social pressure to ostracize the costumed student. Aggressive and dismissive language has included insults to the intelligence of the opponent, wild accusations about his or her character, legitimate threats, and just violently colorful imperatives. For example, "You can't wear that, because you don't know what it's like." Or, "Change that costume, or you will be expelled." Or, "GO SCREW YOURSELF YOU RACIST PIECE OF GARBAGE."

The safe space approach succeeds in very quickly dealing with the immediate problem of a stupid costume. But it does not win a single convert. It may be true that the costumed opponent does not "know what it's like", but he is no more the wiser now than he was before he encountered the safe space. He has certainly been silenced, but that is not a success for the Democratic movement. This costumed "piece of garbage" has not been converted. He has not become a Democratic voter. He is now a seething enemy, silent but lying in wait, ready to strike back at the first political opportunity.

It should be noted here that the use of blackface in a costume can certainly offend. It is arguably disrespectful and tactless. But rejecting a person for their costume is not the same as educating a person about the issue at hand. People do not learn lessons by being socially rejected; they only learn which groups they should now despise.

A major outlet for outreach was shut down in this process. The person-to-person persuasion that often took place at college campuses certainly did not have a 100% success rate. But it did have some rate of success. Some percentage of people were converted through intellectual debate. Some percentage of those went home and converted friends and family. It allowed the liberal message to spread to every part of the country.

But the safe space approach is converting few, if any. It has a 100% percent success rate at shutting people up, but around a 0% success rate of converting anyone. When people go home for the holidays, they do not act as missionaries of the liberal value system. They go home and commiserate with like minded people.

The fact is: if people cannot talk, they cannot be persuaded. If they cannot express their views, you cannot learn how to change their views. I have recruited many people to the Libertarian Party over the last decade, and met others who have recruited ten times as many. We all agree: you have to listen in order to convert. Only by listening can you know where your differences of opinion, usually quite small, actually lie.

If instead, you simply demand that people convert to your belief system because if they do not they are racist, sexist, homophobic trash, you will never understand where the differences of opinion actually lie, let alone how to target and change them. And, perhaps more poignant after this 2016 election, you will be blindsided when all the people you silenced suddenly find their voices at the ballot box.

As a clarification, I am not suggesting that the safe space movement is a bad idea. I am saying that the manner in which it has been implemented has been far from politically strategic. The benefits of such a structure may well outweigh the costs, but for the 2016 election, the safe space movement certainly limited the most important part of the Democratic Party's outreach. In the process of so effectively pushing every distasteful thing below the surface, the progressive movement "cleaned up the streets", but left a writhing underbelly just beneath their feet.

THE SILENCED MAJORITY

As was evident in the example of the college student's costume, the impact of silencing one's opponent is not often the result one might hope for. Unfortunately, this practice of safe space regulations and attacks has been extended far past the boundaries of college campuses, and has reached even into the most inexplicable of places. This overreach exacerbated the feelings of malcontent in progressives' opponents and contributed heavily to the results of the 2016 election.

I witnessed a clear illustration of this at an event in DC last year. This outlandish costume party featured a raunchy comedy show with audience participation antics, all set to a rather obscene soundtrack. Cameras and cellphones were not allowed.

One person got into the spirit of the situation by wearing a red and green novelty Native American head-dress. The stage performer at this particularly uncouth event treated him not as a guest who had made some sort of faux pas, but as a wayward child. She immediately threatened violence if he did not remove the headdress, vaguely hinting at her own part Native American roots as a justification for her outrage. Obviously, he refused to. The party was a far cry from a politically correct event, and, of course, threatening violence to get what you want usually receives a refusal from the opposing side.

Perhaps more importantly, her unmitigated anger made no sense. She was an employee of an establishment that thrived on impropriety, interrupting the inappropriate acts to demand decorum. The headdress man saw this incongruity, the audience saw it, but still the performer continued. She began a barrage of insults, mocking the size of his genitalia, his intelligence level, etc. Many of the guests started getting pretty uncomfortable. After all, the event was a self-proclaimed safe space for comedic impropriety, so they were not expecting to witness such vitriol. The performer was treating the audience member with a total lack of respect or politeness, and was secondarily disrespecting the audience by interrupting the show they had paid to see.

There were plenty of polite ways to handle the situation. The performer clearly did not feel that they were necessary or deserved. Her actions clearly embodied the mindset of, "I am right. If you disagree, you are immoral."

That type of mindset will not convince anyone of anything; it only shuts them up. That guy could have become a convert to the progressive cause over the following days or weeks, but I doubt he did. I'm pretty sure that in the voting booth, he remembered that humiliation. And many others who have suffered from that same aggressive mindset remembered their humiliation and resentment as well.

When you use social pressure or threats to silence all dissenters, it creates the public illusion that you have won. Only the people on your side are speaking; everyone who opposes you now has no public voice. But the problem is that voting is a private act, not a public one. In the privacy of the voting booth, the "immoral" masses find their voice. A silenced majority is still a majority.

VALUE CONFLICTS

When desires conflict, we try to give preference to the more important desire. Fred's desire to not be punched dominates John's desire to punch someone. Amy's desire to play music loud enough to shatter windows is of lower importance than Julie's desire to not have her windows shattered. However, Julie's desire that no one listen to offensive music is lower than Amy's desire to listen to whatever she wants in the privacy of her home.

Recent decades have seen major social, cultural, and legal change. Gay marriage has become legal. Medical marijuana, hemp, and even recreational marijuana have become legal in many states. Many of these changes have reflected the principle of relative value importance.

The desire of gay men and women to enjoy their sexuality, commit to each other, and be able to visit each other in the hospital has been established as more important than the desires of others to not be made uncomfortable. People's desire to smoke marijuana is now considered more important than the desires of others to prevent them from smoking.

While this change is recent, the principle is not new. The past argument for marijuana prohibition often relied on the presumption that marijuana and other drugs would lead to violence. The desire to be kept safe from violence was considered more important than the desire for drug enjoyment.

If an observer did not understand that principle, they would simply think that laws are becoming more pro gay and more pro marijuana. If they extrapolated, they would assume that as time went forward, laws would become more and more pro gay, pro trans, pro marijuana, etc.

But the fact is, much of the drive in these legal movements has come from people who are neither pro-gay nor pro-marijuana. They just objectively consider the balance of desires to need to be adjusted.

For example, many supporters of drug legalization do not use drugs themselves. Many supporters of gay rights are not gay. They simply believe that the desires of gay people to do what they want in private is more important than the desire of others to not be made uncomfortable.

While the battle for gay marriage was raging, many said, "How does someone else being gay and married affect you? How does their marriage in any way threaten your marriage?"

The opposition firmly stated that "gay marriage does threaten the sanctity of straight marriage," but this was soundly defeated. Most people did not believe that gay marriage had any impact on straight marriage at all, and so they felt that the desire to not feel "threatened" in this way mattered less than the ability of all people to pursue personal marital happiness.

These sentiments were often expressed like this: "If two guys want to have sex in their own bedroom, that's their business. If they want to have sex in my bedroom, that's my business." Or: "If someone wants to smoke marijuana in their own homes or businesses, that's their right. If they want to smoke in my home or business, then I have a right to say no."

Many of the more recent changes in law, though, particularly those involving trans rights, have taken a step into a grayer area.

For example, businesses cannot fire people for being trans. Often, people come out as trans while working a job; depending on the nature of the job, this can create an issue for the business owner.

For example, if a computer programmer comes out as trans, that realistically has no possibility of a material effect on a business. No one knows or cares about the personal life or appearance of the person who works on the next Windows security update, or the next iOS update.

On the other hand, if someone works at a daycare and comes out as trans, that could create a major financial danger for the business owner. Many parents simply would not be comfortable with that.

One can argue that the discomfort parents have needs to be changed, and this may be true. However, forcing the business owner to keep the trans daycare teacher

on staff will not change public perception. It will only cause
parents to switch to a competitor, and quite possibly drive
the daycare out of business, or cut substantially into profits
(money available for growth and advertising, etc.).

The result is a new kind of trans-phobia. This is not
an irrational fear of seeing someone who is trans. It is the
rational fear of accidentally hiring someone who is trans, in
a business in which that would pose a financial risk.

Private perception of trans varies significantly,
particularly in the light of increasing numbers of trans
individuals. Many believe that a large number of people are
simply born in a body whose gender does not match their
psychological gender. Others believe that being trans is just
an expression of self hatred or self mutilation. Some have
argued that trans is essentially "the new goth."

Still others have argued that gender itself is a
socially constructed way to limit thought and force people
into pre-existing paths of existence. They believe that while
male and female biological sex exists, that the social genders
around them are entirely fabricated. Those who reject the
gender binary often argue that "gender is the first form of
psychological oppression."

Some even believe that trans is a form of mental
illness. In fact, until 2012, the American Psychiatric
Association classified it as "Gender Identity Disorder".
Even now, in 2016, the World Health Organization

classifies trans as a mental health disorder, but is in the process of declassifying it.

The point is not that trans is good or bad. The point is that given the public perception about it, it poses a real financial threat to many service oriented businesses.

This is obviously most true when people are transitioning. For example, there are male-to-female trans people who look like female supermodels. Having someone like that involved in the public face of any businesses probably will not hurt. On the other hand, someone who is transitioning, halfway between one gender and another, can put customers off, particularly in childcare and related areas.

This obviously creates a conflict of desires. There is the desire of the trans person to express what they consider to be their correct gender. There is the desire of the business owner to make money, not go out of business, and support his family.

Many business owners feel that a trans person can simply dress traditionally during work, and then do whatever they want outside of work. Much like *Mulan*, who dressed like a man in order to join the military, they believe that a trans person can simply fake it during work.

Many trans activists feel that this is an insult to their fundamental identity. They have to go through so much inner struggle, and fight so much social pressure to come out as trans. For them, it is a major achievement. For them to be told to hide this feels like an insult.

Most hardcore progressives I have spoken to believe that the business should just deal with the consequences, and that the right of self expression is more important than the business owner's right to have a working business. Most everyone else I have spoken with disagrees.

But there is a key difference. Most of the hardcore progressives I have discussed this with simply do not see the possibility of another viewpoint to their own. To them, sacrificing a person's business and method of supporting a family is a minuscule price to pay for trans acceptance. They do not see the plight of the business owner at all. Most everyone else at least sees the struggle that the trans community experiences.

Progressives understand that for many, expressing an inner gender is an important form of self-actualization. But they fail to see that a small business owner's business is also an important form of self-actualization. The person who struggles to create a business against all odds, who manages to survive against big and established competitors, views that business as a part of his identity. Forcing him to risk, deform, or entirely sacrifice that part of his identity is likely to turn him into an enemy, and to turn other business owners into sympathetic enemies as well.

Progressives say that if a small daycare fails because customers find a trans day care worker off putting, it is no big deal. The small business owner can just go get a government or corporate job. After all, it is important that someone does not feel trapped in the wrong gender.

But they do not see that for a small business owner to be forced into a government job is just as restrictive as being trapped in the wrong gender. Forcing an entrepreneur into a bureaucracy is trapping him, forcing him to be who he fundamentally does not want to be.

The "trans acceptance above all other considerations" does not go over well with most small business owners. Given that 12 percent of small businesses are sued for wrongful termination, and many more settle out of court, this pro-trans-at-all-costs view alienates many business owners and their families.

SMALL BUSINESSES

According to the government's Small Business Association: "Small businesses make up 99.7% of U.S. employer firms, 64% of net new private-sector jobs, 49.2% of private-sector employment, 42.9% of private-sector payroll, and 46% of private-sector output."

As an entrepreneur, I can tell you that starting small business is an undertaking of love and perseverance. You start out as the unknown little guy, always facing bigger competitors with huge advertising and legal budgets. You have to face one hurdle after another.

Getting customers. Buying equipment. Innovating. You pour your soul into your business.

It is a deep and fundamental part of your identity. I would be much less unsettled if someone changed my ethnicity than if they took away my business.

A small business is created from passion, like a work of art. You make major sacrifices to make it work. You stay up late, carefully choose the appearance of everything. You carefully choose your own clothing to help increase the odds of success. Some business women choose to delay or forego having kids in order to make their businesses succeed.

Many small businesses do not succeed. In fact, within 2 years, about 34 percent of small businesses fail! It takes everything and then some just to survive; it takes limitless perseverance and creativity to make it succeed.

People love their small businesses the way parents love their kids. Or the way non-parents love themselves. After all, a small business is an extension of yourself. So many small businesses are named after the owner, as a deep mark of pride and ownership.

So what's the problem? Unfortunately, the struggle for many small business owners does not end with trans-rights debates. As it turns out, those businesses are also targets of the tyranny of political correctness, the tyranny of delicacy, and the tyranny of entitlement. It has become increasingly common for small businesses to get sued – often by their own employees!

In fact, 13 percent of small businesses get sued by employees, primarily for wrongful termination. This means that the employee felt that they were fired unfairly. According to Human Resources consultant Mary Gorski and Attorney Denise Tataryn, from 1989 to 2009, "wrongful termination lawsuits have risen 260 percent" and "the average cost to settle an employee lawsuit for the small business owner in 2006 rose to $310,845. In 2001, the average cost stood at $130,476" (*Legal Landmines*, 2009).

In fairness, some portion of these wrongful termination suits are probably justified. But a giant portion of them involve what many voters might classify as privileged entitlement. If a small business owner fires an alcoholic employee, they may be sued for wrongful termination (under the Americans with Disabilities Act). An employee may decide to transition genders while employed. The transition can be awkward and drive away customers. For the entrepreneur who carefully adjusted his own wardrobe to make his business have the best chance of success, this seems disrespectful and preposterous.

Some of the more popular bases of claims for wrongful termination are scientifically impossible. Some employees sue small business owners for firing them based on race. Unless they changed race while employed, it is difficult to see how this makes sense. If race was such an issue, it is unlikely that the entrepreneur would have hired the person in the first place, only to fire them later.

Out of fear, or simply because they lack the legal funds, small business owners often just settle out of court. Sometimes entrepreneurs settle because they simply do not have the time for a trial, or do not want their customers to be subpoenaed. Furthermore, those that do go through the trouble of a trial often lose. According to the Los Angeles Times, "If an employment lawsuit goes to trial, plaintiffs [employees] are more likely to win 67 percent of the time in state courts and 63 percent in federal courts."

Small businesses are even targeted and sued by lawyers and serial plaintiffs. After all, they are easy targets. They do not have the giant legal teams of McDonald's or Microsoft.

In one family-owned restaurant in California, the owner replaced a mirror that was destroyed by vandals. The new mirror was slightly smaller, and ended up being placed two inches higher than what is specified in the Americans with Disabilities Act. The plaintiff sued the owner for 27 counts spread over a 3 month period.

Interestingly, the same plaintiff and lawyer targeted two other nearby restaurants for similar claims. A law initially designed to protect the disabled has turned some into tyrants. Consideration was transformed into political correctness, which was deformed into legal tyranny.

Finally, small business owners are denied the right to choose whether or not to provide a service. Many small, Christian bakeries have been forced to create cakes for same sex weddings. They have literally been coerced to use their hard earned skill to engage in an act with which they disagree. For them, it is no different than a Jewish baker forced to bake a Nazi a cake. The difference, of course, is that Nazis are the old kind of bully, the kind that operates from a position of strength and aggression. They say, "I am so strong, that I will force you to do what I want you to."

The same sex couples coercing the baker are the new kind of bullies, operating from a position of weakness and entitlement. They say, "I am vulnerable and need protection from bigotry. If you do not do what I say, the government will force you to do what I want."

There is no major difference in methodology. The main difference is in perception: those who refuse to bake the Nazi cake are seen as heroes. Those who refuse to bake the same sex marriage cake are seen as homophobic bigots.

In my business (an education business), we are happy to serve anyone who can pay. But there are plenty of services we refuse to offer. For example, we refuse to teach Common Core math, because I consider it inefficient and ineffective. If someone tried to force me to do so with the threat of imprisonment, then I would just go to prison.

While I do not have the same beliefs, I understand that for many religious wedding bakers, their views on what comprises a proper wedding is just as important as the right way to teach math is to me. I might not share their views, but I understand what it means to have strong views. And I know that forcing people to violate their own beliefs is an unconscionable and deeply personal violation.

This new politically elevated class does not get that. To them, a small business is just some job you go to. The fact that people work so hard to be able to contribute by doing something they truly love is not understood by many progressives, and is regularly devalued or dismissed.

The resentment against those bullies of weakness has grown in accordance with their increasing abuse of power. It becomes unconscious resentment against the disabled, those who have different gender identities, etc. Those small business owners are sick of living under a tyranny of weakness, walking around on eggshells, afraid to offend someone, afraid to violate the ADA.

So when Trump, like a bull in a china shop, mocked a disabled reporter, some well hidden part of them might have actually felt relief. When Trump chose as his running mate Mike Pence, who fought for the rights of entrepreneurs, they may have been perfectly happy. They did not say anything aloud; they had learned not to. But they still felt recognized and protected by Trump and Pence far more than they have been under the Democrats.

While Democratic voters saw Pence as anti-gay, small business owners saw him as someone who finally stood up for their natural rights. While Democratic voters saw Trump as unconscionably boorish, small business owners saw him attacking the political correctness that gave rise to stifling and frightening employment law or the equally terrifying Americans with Disabilities Act.

All of these laws, and their abuses, have helped turn the political tides of this country. If progressives want to maintain their political agenda, they will need to adapt to the largely overlooked needs of small business owners, among countless others.

THE UNCOMPROMISING VIEW

The "Our Way at All Costs" mentality, which leads to political backlash, is not just an issue of LGBTQ and disabled rights. Progressives have made the same strategic error with abortion, and conservatives have made the same error with medical marijuana.

In *The Leviathan*, Thomas Hobbes writes, "there is no way for any man to secure himself so reasonable as anticipation; that is, by force, or wiles, to master the persons of all men he can so long till he see no other power great enough to endanger him." In other words, in order to protect yourself from threat, you often pursue more power over others than you might otherwise want.

This happens often in politics. People fight battles far ahead of where they are actually worried about being threatened. As George W. Bush said, "It's better to fight them there than here."

As an example, most people in America are pro-choice. That means they believe that a woman has the right to get an abortion.

However, a pretty high percentage of America is pro-life; they believe that abortion should be illegal. A good portion of those people make exceptions for cases of rape and incest, considering it cruel to force a woman to bring to term a baby conceived in rape.

But the most relevant question in abortion right now is not whether or not it should be legal. The question is whether it should be tax-supported. In other words: is it right to force people to pay to support an act they find morally unacceptable?

It is a tricky area of tax policy in general. Pacifists still have to pay taxes for war. Environmentalists still have to pay taxes for oil subsidies.

The political views are all over the map, but many pro-choice people do not support forcing people to pay for abortions. They believe that women should be allowed to have abortions, that others should be allowed to voluntarily donate to support that, but that people should not be compelled to support them through taxes.

Even many progressives agree. In fact, they do not fight for government funding for abortion because they consider it particularly justified or necessary. The only reason they are fighting on that point is that they believe that if government funding for abortion is eliminated, the overall right to abortion will be challenged next.

But many independent groups oppose federal funding for abortion, and the current progressive strategy is alienating them. Although roughly 60% of Libertarians are pro-choice, approximately 0% support federal funding for abortion. By "fighting them there instead of here", the progressive movement has alienated its natural allies. Instead of fighting on a strong position that would rally many to its cause, it has fought on an issue where there is little support outside of the guaranteed support of hardcore progressives.

To advance a progressive agenda on abortion, the movement could instead focus on eliminating mandatory pre-abortion counseling, which is also unpopular. This would also involve providing additional protection for abortion, but this time from a popular position. By fighting against something already unpopular, the progressive move-ment could win over independents. Instead, by fighting in

favor of unpopular federal funding, the progressive movement is turning away independent voters.

Some conservatives have made the same error with
medical marijuana. Those who oppose legalizing medical
marijuana do not really have a strong opposition to cancer
patients being able to reduce their pain. They believe that
medical marijuana will be the first domino, and will be
followed by recreational marijuana, and then the complete
legalization of all drugs.

But their strategy of fighting everything "there
instead of here" has made them look cruel, out of touch,
paranoid, and even stupid. The initial fights about medical
marijuana made the opponents to its legalization look
heartless. They lost social credibility in that fight. Then,
when the fight moved to recreational marijuana, the conservatives had already lost too much social capital. The world
viewed them as unfeeling and out of touch.

Trump's stance on abortion, while less popular that
Hillary's, did not hurt him much politically. People predicted
that the most Trump would be able to do would be to eliminate federal funding for abortion, which they were fine with.

It is possible those predictions will turn out to
be wrong. Abortion may be entirely banned by 2018. But
people vote based on predictions, not hindsight.

INSULARITY

The Democratic belief that the rights of trans people to dress as they choose is more important than the financial security of small businesses has alienated many. Shifting the abortion debate to federal funding has also alienated many. While these stances were created more by the movement than by the Clinton campaign, Hillary certainly paid the price.

Many of these viewpoints, by the way, are not coming from deliberate insensitivity. They are coming from insularity. In DC, where 38 percent of workers are employed by the government, many more work for huge government contractors, and others work for giant corporations, they simply do not have any idea what it is like to work for a business whose financial security could be threatened at all, let alone by the presence of a trans employee.

For that matter, even small businesses in big cities would be less likely to be financially threatened by an openly trans employee, given that being pro-trans is currently politically fashionable. (Childcare businesses would be the obvious exception.)

But in many parts of the country and in many industries outside of the big coastal cities, a trans employees choice to dress for their chosen gender can threaten the financial security of a business.

Incidentally, it does not have to be that way. This is a social issue that pro-trans people can easily fix financially by actively patronizing businesses that hire trans employees. That way, instead of a trans employee being a financial liability, the employee would be a financial asset. Instead of mere social acceptance, trans people would be welcomed with huge economic demand. Imagine if the Hollywood actors who supported Hillary voluntarily promoted trans-friendly businesses, instead of promoting laws that require grudging acceptance of trans employees. Trans people would very quickly be the most sought after group in American employment.

In order to regain value dominance, the progressive movement must grow past using laws and government to compel obedience to progressive values. This method only creates resentment. Instead, it should find ways to use its considerable financial and cultural resources to shape values through non-coercive methods.

FORCE AND CULTURE

Many progressives understand the futility of using force to spread culture. For example, they realize that forcing the entire Middle East to convert to Christianity is unlikely to be effective.

The same is true of American culture in general. American attempts at setting up pro-American govern-ments in the Middle East have been largely ineffective.

Progressives often argue that "you can't bomb people into agreeing with you."

However, in the absence of coercion, American culture spreads. American popular culture and ideals have spread across continents.

Some of the mechanisms are economically motivated. If, for example, a businessman in Malaysia wants to sell products in America, he must learn about American culture. So must his copywriters, graphic designers, operations team, etc. For purely economic reasons, he must learn about American culture.

Of course, he does not have to agree to any of it. And the worldwide consumers of American culture do not have to choose American music, film, and literature.

American culture spreads quickly because it just has a lot of good ideas - literary, political, and social. Even when American culture is actively blocked, it still spreads. Our culture even spreads in China, where Facebook and other social media sites are banned.

American culture is rejected primarily in parts of the world in which attempts are made to force our culture and political ideas on groups of people.

The progressive movement understands this. They know that culture is best spread without direct force or the threat of force. They know that threats only breed resentment.

But the progressive movement must realize this is equally true within the borders of America. Encouraging trans acceptance without coercion will build allies; using coercion to force acceptance will, and already has, created enemies.

Some say that noncoercive trans acceptance will take longer. But the reality is that coercive trans acceptance will take forever. The illusion can be created by forcing compliance, but the resentment created will continually backfire. The 2016 election is one small example.

SEALING THE ECHO CHAMBER

The Democratic echo chamber was exacerbated by the extension of the safe space movement into interactions between acquaintances. Among acquaintances, progressives saw not potential converts or peers coming from different backgrounds and perspectives but an immoral filth that had infiltrated their inner circles. A politically self-destructive purge commenced.

During the Clinton campaign, I routinely saw social media posts to the effect of, "If you support Trump, go ahead and unfriend me," usually with far more colorful language. Clinton supporters were literally cutting off connection with potential converts. They were surrounding themselves with only people who already agreed with their own personal beliefs.

This course of action actually got them more fired up. They believed their cause was good; all of their friends believed this too. They could not hear the opposition anymore because they had shut it out completely, and so they believed that Hillary would win. Each of their votes was cast with more gusto.

But there were not more votes where it mattered. By isolating themselves, Democratic activists nearly eliminated their entire outreach, and wildly overestimated their candidate's popularity.

POST ELECTION ECHOES

After the election, I, like many, took to Facebook to discuss the results. I responded to a friend's anti-Trump post that discussed allegations of sexual assault. I questioned the use of the word "rapist" to describe him. Within a few messages of political disagreement, one person had repeatedly told me to take a hike (in far more creative language), another announced that they were going to cry. I doubt it was because of any aggressiveness in the way I disagreed (there was not any that I could detect, and certainly none on par with the responses). It was the fact that I had disagreed.

I have pretty thick skin, so I continued the dialogue. But most reasonable people would have shut up pretty quickly. After the election, many people did just that. More friendships were destroyed or abandoned, further limiting future outreach. The Echo Chamber was still in place; vitriolic attacks came to almost all whose opinions differed from the accepted, liberal views.

To be fair, a few were completely polite and willing to take the time to explain their viewpoint. They addressed the ideas, rather than switching to personal attacks. But the quickest on the draw, and the most frequent posters, were those who preferred obscenity and literal crying. It is not an effective way to win converts.

I feel it is important to note that I do not believe all humans should be heartless robots who have no emotions. I believe people were in pain after the election, and crying is a natural reaction to pain. But crying over every reminder that some people disagree with you is a terrible political strategy, and will not help the progressive movement win new converts.

TRIGGERED

One increasingly common word in progressive culture is "triggered." This refers to being emotionally traumatized by an insensitive reference to a topic about which the triggered person is emotionally vulnerable. The insensitive reference triggers a post-traumatic emotional response.

While this word undoubtedly came from good intentions, it has now essentially come to mean "disagreed with." And when a person is triggered (disagreed with), it has become socially acceptable for that person to devolve into hysterics and profanity. Obviously, this completely destroys the potential for positive outreach. You can only convert people who disagree with you. And converting people usually involves delving into personal issues. When you make that whole area of discussion off limits, it restricts the intensity and effectiveness of any kind of conversion oriented outreach. The most you get is social conformity, not true agreement.

THE ALT-RIGHT

These feelings of being forgotten, disrespected, and silenced have led to the explosive popularity of the alt-right.

The alt-right is a vaguely defined conservative movement whose major focus is on being as offensive as possible. They intentionally say racist and sexist things that even they often do not believe. On the topic of whether the alt-right is racist, Allum Bokhari and Milo Yiannopoulos, prominent figures in this leaderless movement, state, "No more than death metal devotees in the 80s were actually

Satanists." Other key figures, on the other hand, argue that the entire message is extremely serious, and should be taken literally. It should be noted, though, that some key figures in the alt-right are people of color themselves.

The alt-right's focus is on the heroic masculine (i.e. the kind of alpha male so powerful he cannot be silenced), white tribal identity, and a massive opposition to safe spaces and "feelings first".

The existence of the alt-right does not need much explaining. There have always been groups and individuals who like being offensive. White nationalism has existed for decades.

But the huge popularity of this movement, particularly among millennials, does warrant an explanation. Trump's victory may have made them a bit bolder, but it did not create the movement.

How can a group whose ideas went out of style decades ago be suddenly so explosively popular? Why are their leaders drawing crowds at universities, including far left universities?

When people are silenced, they act out. They fight back. They try to intellectually and culturally destroy the thing that is trying to silence them. Those who feel silenced at college are happy to have anyone stand up and refuse to be silenced on any topic at all.

When people are not allowed to speak, sometimes they yell instead. The alt-right movement's popularity indicates the extent to which people are feeling silenced on many college campuses.

And unlike the progressive movement, which is focusing on silencing opposition, the alt-right is aggressively doing outreach. They are intentionally keeping their principles loose and ill-defined, in order to have a wide reach. They are debating and working to convince people to join them, so their numbers have grown.

My guess: as with most ill-defined, anti-establishment movements, it will probably be co-opted by a well organized, pro-establishment movement. The Tea Party was co-opted by the GOP. Tea Party voters supported Mitt Romney, one of the most pro-establishment politicians in American history. Similarly, the Occupy movement was co-opted by actual government employee unions. It is hard to even imagine a more pro-establishment organization that government employee unions.

An ill defined movement without clear principles can be co-opted.

Depending on what Trump does in office, this may have already happened to the alt-right movement, which obviously supported Trump. Right now, he is talking about leaving NATO and shutting down the Federal Department of Education, which are arguably anti-establishment. He is also talking about several pro-establishment ideas, as well as those that are hard to categorize, like building a wall and deporting illegal immigrants. If Trump ends up only solidifying the status quo, it will indicate that the anti-establishment alt-right was successfully co-opted by the Trump campaign.

Of course, the alt-right should not be seen as a primary cause of Clinton's defeat. It is a symptom of a larger movement that caused Clinton's defeat. In 2016, alt-right supporters were a numerically small movement, but they expressed in an aggressive and distorted way the frustration that a numerically large group felt.

Manufacturers know that for every one person who writes a complaint letter about an aspect of a product, at least 100 people disliked it but did not bother to write the letter. Similarly, for every person in the alt-right, there are hundreds who are fed up with the current interpretation of politically correct culture. While those hidden millions may not have been willing to reject social norms so aggressively, they were willing to vote.

The Clinton campaign's failure to recognize this, and to take any measures to respond, contributed to their unexpected loss.

THE MOST DEVASTATING TRUTH

As I'm writing this, many progressives are having total meltdowns. Some are crying. College students are taking off class, and Universities are allowing and encouraging it.

I do not think that this is because they are sore losers. Some of it may come from concerns over racism or bigotry. A lot of it is because they have realized that they simply do not know who around them supported Trump. They know that those people have learned to hide, blend in, and not reveal anything. But Democrats do not know who around them to try to convert (or eject from their safe spaces).

The largest issue, though, is coming from the gradual realization that their entire value system is now vulnerable, because their entire method of social control is now vulnerable. Their method of value dominance has come to rely, not on superior arguments, or any arguments at all, but on a huge numerical advantage.

And they just realized that they do not have one.

SMUG AND DISMISSIVE

UNSTRATEGIC DISMISSIVENESS

In politics, it often makes sense to attack opponents. Making the other side look worse encourages voters to switch to your side, and reinforces your voters' belief that they have definitely chosen the right candidate.

To be polite, people in politics often say that they oppose all the negative campaigning in politics. But that is just to be polite. Negative campaigning has been part of politics since Ancient Greece, and it is not going away any time soon.

While it makes sense to attack the other candidate, it rarely makes sense to attack the supporters of the other candidate. If your intention is to convince opposing voters to change their minds and vote for you, you want them to hate their current first choice candidate. You do not want them to hate you.

Even worse than attacking the specific supporters of other candidates is attacking the general category of the supporters. That alienates not only current supporters, but also other people in that category.

For example, in 2012, if Romney had said, "We need to fight against all these black people who support Obama," it would have brought out 100% of the black vote and 100% of the minority vote to vote against him.

On September 9, 2016, at a New York fundraiser, Hillary said: "To just be grossly generalistic, you could put half of Trump's supporters into what I call the 'basket of deplorables. Right? The racist, sexist, homophobic, xenophobic, Islamaphobic, you name it. And unfortunately, there are people like that."

"Unfortunately there are people like that," literally says, "Those people should not exist." No one likes to be told that they should not exist. Minorities know, gays know, women know that this is about the worst thing you can say to a person. And everyone who had ever been called racist, sexist, homophobic, xenophobic, or Islamaphobic, whether the title was apt or not, felt totally rejected by Hillary Clinton.

Furthermore, each of those terms is a pejorative for fairly common behavior, and many people who are not "deplorable" have in fact been called these things plenty of times. For example, a man who wants to marry a housewife, who does not work and cares for the kids, is almost always considered sexist. For that matter, even a woman who wants to get married and be a stay at home mom could be derided for her sexist belief that a woman's place is in the home.

A person who believes that marriage should only be between a man and a woman, (for example Bill Clinton, who signed the Defense of Marriage act, or Obama, who just a few years ago supported only civil unions), probably has been called homophobic. Many supporters of American foreign military policy in the Middle East (including Hillary Clinton) have been called Islamophobic. So have those who oppose refugee immigration for economic rather than ethnic reasons. Those who oppose illegal immigration, including the entire Department of Homeland Security and quite a bit of state level law enforcement, have been called xenophobic.

Many of those voters listened for years to people telling them that their way of life placed them in some -ist category, and then they listened to Hillary tell them that they should not exist. For whom do you think they voted?

Of course, these are all examples of times when the insults slung around are not true, but they can still be painful psychologically and politically. When Hillary made that deplorables speech, those who had been called by those pejorative terms, either accurately or inaccurately, felt entirely dismissed and rejected. Many religious people remain uncomfortable with recent cultural changes in our society, and they felt insulted and shut out. Even military service members have been called Islamaphobic so many times that Hillary may as well have been talking about them.

Recognize here that, while it may be a horrible thing for a person to be truly racist, sexist, etc., there are far too many people incorrectly given these labels, and so Hillary's language was too vague and broad. Attacking a specific racist group, like the Ku Klux Klan, makes sense. Almost all people called KKK members are actually KKK members. But attacking the vaguely defined group of "anyone ever called racist, sexist, homophobic, etc." is politically unwise.

Hillary either directly or indirectly attacked too large a percentage of the population. She made Democrats feel good because everyone likes to feel like they're better than the "other", but she alienated millions.

THAT'S NOT WHAT SHE MEANT

Clinton supporters quickly point out that the afore-mentioned groups were not who she meant. She did not mean to attack the entire Christian base or the stay at home moms or the men and women in the military. Hillary only meant the big, mean, aggressive skinheads with swastika tattoos. That may be true, but what she meant and what America heard are still two different things, and America voted based on what it heard, not on what she meant.

Now of course, candidates sometimes say things that are perceived as offensive, and in those times, they

apologize and are able to continue their campaign; one
poor comment does not usually decide an entire election. Other candidates have made mistakes like this one.
Why was Hillary's comment so much worse than, for
example, Obama's suggestion that conservatives "cling to
their guns and religion"?

With Obama, he did not say that it's too bad that
religious people exist. He himself goes to church. Nor
did he use direct pejoratives. For example, he did not call
religious people "addicts to backwards superstitions" or
anything. It was written off as a gaffe.

Also, and far more importantly, he directly
apologized. He showed that he understood the struggles
of the people he had insulted: "I said when you're bitter,
you turn to what you can count on. So people vote about
guns, or they take comfort from their faith and their family
and their community. Now, I didn't say it as well as I
should have. If I worded things in a way that made people
offended, I deeply regret that."

Note that he apologized, made every indication
he would not repeat the mistake, and showed that he cared
about the struggles of those whom he had (supposedly
inadvertently) insulted.

On the other hand, Clinton said: "Last night I was
'grossly generalistic,' and that's never a good idea. I regret
saying 'half' – that was wrong."

In other words, she apologized for the mathematical inaccuracy, but not for the overall principle that those who oppose gay marriage (e.g. Bill Clinton a few years ago) should not exist. She apologized for making a mathematically inaccurate statement. Her concern seemed to be with being right, so she apologized for the technical error.

She did not try to win over those she had dismissed. She showed no compassion for their struggle, no interest in their needs and wants. It was a perfect opportunity. Everyone in her campaign, and everyone on earth, knew that her biggest public image problem was a perception of arrogance. She could have made a heartfelt speech, showing humility and compassion, and won over millions. It could have gone something like this:

"Last night, I said something I should not have. In the heat of a political debate, I inadvertently insulted many Americans. Right now, many of you feel dismissed and unappreciated. For that, I sincerely apologize. I want you to know this: if I am elected, even if you did not vote for me, I will be your president too. I know that there have been changes over the last years that have been difficult, some that you do not agree with. Instead of insulting you, I should be doing my best to listen to your concerns. I deeply regret dismissing you. While we may not agree on everything, I can promise that I will never stop listening to you."

I'm sure that her multimillion dollar staff of speech writers could have come up with something better, but even the above would have gotten the job done.

Of course, one off-color comment was not the crux of Hillary's loss. It was just a striking symptom of a much more pervasive and detrimental mindset of dismissiveness and superiority. People want to feel listened to, not railroaded, insulted, and dismissed. And Hillary never seemed to be listening, nor did her ardent, smug followers.

WHAT ABOUT TRUMP?

What about Trump? Didn't he make a huge mistake by insulting the parents of a fallen Muslim American soldier? Didn't that insult extend to other Muslim American soldiers as well? Wouldn't that have hurt him?

It almost certainly did. It made him look boorish and socially out of touch. It was a bad move.

Trump had a clever, partial apology: he later referred to the soldier as a hero. This probably appeased many in the military.

He did not apologize to the parents of the soldier however. I doubt this was a particularly smart political move; it is pretty clear that he completely mishandled that situation. But he insulted a lower percentage of the population that Clinton had. It was a race to the bottom of political strategy, a question of who could be the most self-destructively rude. Hillary won.

DEPTH OF SMUGNESS

Smugness turns people off. Apparently not recognizing this, in the most critical moments of the election, the Clinton campaign took smugness to a whole new level. They announced to the world where they were holding their victory party: below a literal glass ceiling in New York. They had fireworks standing by, and the New York City fire department on alert. Obviously, this made her look unbelievably smug and arrogant.

There's nothing wrong with planning a victory party. However, when you come across as smugly certain of victory, it can rub people the wrong way. A few words of humility could have gone a long way. By the way, I mean actual humility, not the "I am humbled to vote for myself" phoniness that she actually gave. That may have been the most blatantly insincere line in the entire campaign, and it could not have come at a worse time.

Throughout the campaign, Hillary's supporters treated her as the obvious, morally right choice, and Trump as the morally wrong one. Trump supporters were considered idiots, and were treated as though they deserved no respect or common decency. Urban, liberal values were proclaimed as having superseded all rural 'values' (which were completely dismissed as unnecessary to take note of or understand). And of course, after the accusations of sexual assault and the damning video evidence of "locker room talk" came out against Trump, The Hillary campaign pointedly switched their strategy to winning the senate; they clearly believed they had the presidential election fully secured.

It is important to note that when people work hard, others generally like to see them succeed. When people smugly claim that they will win no matter what, others generally want to see that person fall flat on his (or in this case her) smug face.

It is also very difficult for many people to stomach voting for someone who acts in such a way. While touting racism as the reason for Hillary's loss, her supporters seem to be blind to the simple fact that Hillary's smugness was highly unlikeable, and that factored heavily into the election results.

HILLARY'S SUPPORTERS' SMUGNESS

Hillary's supporters were equally smug. Many had already registered for her inauguration day celebration on Facebook. The day before the election, thousands of Hillary supporters on social media had written comments like, "No matter who wins tomorrow, let's accept it and move forward."

It could have been a genuine desire to put a divisive election in the past in a show of true sportsmanship. But the evidence suggests otherwise. Many who had posted such comments gave violently angry outbursts once the results came out. The "let's accept the results and move forward nicely" quickly turned into the "Not My President" protests.

It was not a particularly flattering combination. It made "let's be nice after the election" now seem to actually mean, "When we win, shut up and accept it."

In the aftermath of the election, a video circulated from Seriously.tv. Based on the opening, I thought Democrats had finally learned to take other viewpoints seriously. But my hopes were misplaced.

The video opens with the presenter saying, "Trump Supporters: I love you. And I mean that. I'm sorry you have been led to believe that your problems have been caused by immigrants, Muslims, people of color, LGBTQ folk, and PC culture."

Translation: "Trump Supporters: I'm sorry you're so stupid that you can't see reality."

While that type of passive aggressive response is understandable after such a major loss, it is only driving potential converts further and further away. Despite the "I love you" opening, it does not convey, "I respect you" or "I want to understand you." It is more, "I barely tolerate your stupidity, and will never listen to you, or debate you." It is

just another way to shut people up, rather than figuring
out how to win them over.

RURAL AMERICA

What does urban America think of rural America? On
a good day, those who live in cities view rural America
with condescending nostalgia. The rest of the time, urban
Americans look at rural Americans with disdain. Urban
Americans consider rural culture backwards, irrelevant, or
entirely nonexistent. When urban Americans are feeling
nice, we look at rural Americans as our cultural ancestors.
Otherwise, we see them as cultural deadweight.

The pervasive assumption is that those who live in
the country somehow cannot survive in the city. That is the
only possible reason that someone would reject city life in
favor of rural life. This is of course not true, many people
have absolutely no desire to live in urban areas. But this is
how many people view the situation.

From this rejection of rural values has come an
economic rejection. Attitudes and policy seems to state
that urban poverty matter while rural poverty does not.
Economic policies that lead to rural unemployment are
seen as having essentially no casualties. When those of us in
cities hear about rural unemployment, the initial thought is,
"No problem, now they can finally get new skills and move

beyond their backwards way of life." Or, "So? They can just move to a city and get a job there."

Before I got involved in national politics, I unfortunately followed that mindset. Now, having met many more people from rural America, and having spent more time "out in the boondocks" myself, I have begun to understand that rural America is not the past. It is just as much the present as urban America, with cultures just as deep and varied, and with a work ethic just as strong.

Economically, rural America is just as important, if not more important, than urban America. If all federal departments vanished tomorrow, that would cause far less turmoil than if 25% of our agricultural output vanished. We can survive without investment banks and Hollywood. We cannot survive without food and heat.

The cultural and economic dismissal of rural America has led to resentment and frustration. Some of that frustration has turned ugly, as frustration often does. Some has been transformed into racism and Islamophobia. But a lot of what looks like Islamophobia is not really Islamophobia. When your government is looking to shut down coal jobs, but is completely willing to find places for 60,000 refugees, you're going to feel resentment. It is not because you hate all Muslims. It is because you're being treated unfairly.

The Trump campaign reached out to these people, making one stop after another in small towns. The Clinton campaign ignored those areas, seeing them as unwinnable anyway. This of course compounded the problem. She was saying that if a group is not likely to vote for her, it was not worth her time to talk to them.

While Clinton avoided Republican strongholds, Trump actually pursued Democratic strongholds aggressively. He engaged in active outreach to black Americans, even though they traditionally vote Democratic. Imagine how insulted black Americans would have been if Trump did zero outreach to minority communities. Clinton made that mistake with rural America.

The fact is, she could have won over a major part of rural America had she put in the effort. Instead, she kept concentrating on her urban strongholds, preaching increasingly aggressively to her own choir. She further alienated them with her "deplorables" speech. That speech came from a deep certainty that urban, liberal values were absolutely right, and anything else was absolutely wrong. It further showed that she was out of touch with the real concerns of most of America. She could not see that much of the perceived Islamophobia was economic resentment. She did not see that much of the rejection of urban values came from feeling culturally dismissed by urban America.

I do not have nearly the political experience or the massive advisory staff of Hillary Clinton. But even I could see the underlying issues in my discussions with those from rural America. Everyone could see it. The press could see it. Trump could see it.

The only possibilities were that Hillary was obtuse or indifferent. Her air of intellectual arrogance made the former seem unlikely, so the only conclusion that rural America could make was that she simply did not care.

Instead of ignoring rural America in her campaign, she should have gone after rural America. They could have been won over with respect. Instead, she dismissed them with insults. Rural America voted for Trump in droves. They were tired of being treated, culturally and politically, as second class citizens.

"UNEDUCATED" WHITE VOTERS

Rural America received far more attention in the wake of the election results. Unfortunately, the attention was worse than being ignored.

Since the election, the press has fixated on the fact the areas with "uneducated" white voters favored Trump. Specifically, it seems that white men with high school degrees but not college degrees supported Trump. These groups of people have been regularly ignored, cast aside, and often mocked for their stupidity, their lack of initiative, and even their lack of understanding about their own lives and values. It has been said that these backwards people do not understand their own religions or political views at all, and that's why they're so easily led down the path of the "evil" right. Throughout the campaign months, and for years before, these groups were insulted by many liberal voters. In the post-election madness, those same voters have only solidified the classist divide that kept them from winning the 2016 election.

So what is the "problem" with the working class? Some members of the press have taken the more nuanced view that many of these people feel left behind by the modern economy. Their skills are primarily mechanical, and demand for those skills is decreasing. Some of that decrease in demand has come from automation; some has come from outsourcing. The skills are not inherently economically valueless, but many businesses have found alternative ways to address the demand for those skills.

Consider those people, who have valuable skills but are losing their jobs due to a changing economy. Now imagine what they see when they look at the political landscape. They see an entire other group whose skills are not in economic demand. The other group's skills may be more prestigious, but no one is willing to pay for them in the open market. This other group is not suffering, or being left behind, though. This group is treated like royalty at the expense of the working class.

The second group is the "overeducated" College Class. The economic demand for their skills did not suddenly decrease. It was just never that big in the first place. That group's work is not being produced overseas; no one would bother. There just is no major intrinsic economic demand for the products of that group's labor.

If the working class's sin is not enough school, the College Class's sin is too much. They are college graduates at the least, but often hold higher degrees. They may major in something with accepted pragmatic value, like biology, or something without it, like comparative literature.

When demand for these skills is low, or when a person simply prefers to apply their skills to not-in-demand academic research rather than teaching, commercial research, or even in-demand academic research, the government creates subsidies to increase demand. These can be direct research grants, or indirect research grants resulting from the heavy taxpayer funding of colleges. Most of this indirect funding comes through loan subsidies and grants.

In other words, if you are of the privileged College Class, you are now protected from the laws of economics. You want to research biology, but the free market does not need that many biology researchers? No problem. The government will create research grants and jobs to allow you to pursue your personal interest. The National Institutes of Health support about 27,500 researchers per year. This is over and above the researchers employed by the pharmaceutical industry, the biotechnology industry, the agricultural industry, etc.

Obviously, this does not end with biology. The National Endowment for the Humanities has a budget of 167 million dollars. The National Endowment for the Arts has a budget of 146 million dollars. That goes to fund research and exploration of the arts and humanities for which the open market has insufficient economic demand.

When you see this from the perspective of a man or woman who works two, or even three physically demanding jobs, just to somehow manage to buy food and housing for their families, you can see where the resentment might originate.

Note that the free market has plenty of demand for these academic areas, ranging from ticket sales for plays and museums, to commercial art sales, to demand for literature and nonfiction. That marketplace includes the huge demand for films, documentaries, and writers. But if that gigantic and growing demand is not enough for you, the government steps in, provides grants, and allows you to pursue your interests.

The government also provides billions of dollars of indirect and direct aid to research universities. There, professors pursue their interests in subjects ranging from comparative literature to ethnomusicology. Often, this research is not in any economic demand at all. But unlike the high school graduate, the college professor is part of the privileged class. He does not have to be economically useful.

If you are a skilled factory worker, but there is no economic demand for your skills, you just suffer. If you are an anthropology major, and there is no economic demand for your skills, the government creates research grants to allow you to pursue that interest. If you are a biologist, but there is insufficient market demand for biologists, the government will create a grant to allow you to pursue your interest in biology.

Here, in Washington, D.C., you can really see what grant culture is like. Many people make comfortable livings just writing grant proposals! There are so many grants available that there are often grants for which no one applies. The agencies advertise the grants, free money to pursue your hobby, but still no one claims them. The government makes sure that those of the privileged class, those with college educations, will always be able to pursue their interests.

Capitalism can be brutal. Those who do not adapt often feel its sting. But today's privileged class never feels that sting. When the economic demand for their interests goes away (or never existed), the government creates artificial demand for those interests.

I understand that there are many interpretations of the above facts. Some say that the research that college professors do (most of which goes completely unread and uncited by anyone for decades) is highly necessary for the pursuit of knowledge for knowledge's sake. Some say that it is the government funded research that is most likely to give us cures for obscure diseases, or government funded art that will give us the next Picasso. This may be true, but the point here is that it is not how rural Americans see it. They do not get cushy jobs pursuing their hobbies; they are barely making ends meet. To the "uneducated" white working class, carving out a reasonable living means more than the study of Latin or sociology, and Democrats need to recognize this fact if they want to understand why they lost.

THE MONEY

Contrary to popular, Democratic belief, high school educated middle America is not made up of morons. They can see the income tax taken out of their diminished paychecks. They can see the sales tax they pay on every purchase. Those who work in manufacturing see the hidden taxes, where the raw materials used in finished products are taxed separately and then taxed again once the final product is sold. They know that they are working hard, and that much of their labor is going to fund the intellectual hobbies and pursuits of the privileged classes.

The modern economy has left behind both the privileged classes and those with expertise in manufacturing. The free market seems to have insufficient demand for both. In pure capitalism, both would suffer. In pure socialism, both would get the same treatment.

But in reality, only one group actually suffers. The other goes blithely on.

Clinton's Free College Education for all, which some analysts thought would have helped her among high-school educated white men, almost certainly backfired. To them, it was just a way to say, "Pay for everyone's college with your taxes, and then pay for the graduates to pursue their hobbies for life."

And as we have discussed, those colleges are now becoming "safe spaces" rather than places of critical thinking and learning. These men had already heard from the Clinton campaign that off color jokes between friends were no longer okay. Why would they want to be forced to subsidize an expansion of that "safe space" culture?

Those high-school graduates, since they did not starve to death right after high school, must have at some point had some economically desired skill. It must have involved creating something useful. They know what economic usefulness looks like, even if they are struggling at the moment. And they know what economic uselessness looks like.

Attempting to bribe them into joining that culture was bound to backfire.

OTHER PRIVILEGED CLASSES

It is hard for those who produce things of value to tolerate the financial success of those who produce...nothing. Investment bankers are particularly hated for this reason. A man who works hard all day building a house and comes home to a frozen dinner is bound to resent the person who works all day moving money around, producing nothing, and dines at a five star restaurant.

But such is the character of many working class Americans that even when jealous, they do not begrudge people the money that they earned, even if it seems earned too easily and too detached from production. They say, "It doesn't seem totally fair, but I guess you earned it."

The 2008 Wall Street bailout represented a fundamental transformation. Investment bankers were no longer just people who were good at some fancy if non-productive economics. They were people who were bad at it. They failed at it. Their skills were proven to be not just economically useless, but economically devastating.

But did those investment bankers suffer? Did they lose their homes? Did the banks foreclose on them? Did they lose their jobs? Did their standards of living change at all?

No. They just became another privileged class. The Wall Street Bailout ensured that they kept their posh lifestyles despite literally failing economically. The skill of being moronically incompetent at investing has never been in any kind of economic demand, and yet it was rewarded by the government. Goldman Sachs even turned a profit from the entire situation!

The high school educated men heard the arguments, that the money had to go to the investment banks so that it could get to the rest of the economy. But again, those men are not morons. They knew that there had to have been ways to get the money to everyone else while skipping over those banks. There had to have been some way that involved those investment bankers having to sell their homes, and taking their kids out of private schools. They could have been made to suffer for their economic worthlessness, but that was not how the government did it.

They saw that the government allowed the entire manufacturing sector of the economy to leave America. But they only allowed one New York investment bank to fail. Anyone can see the unfairness in that.

And then they saw Hillary, herself a member of that same privileged class. They saw that she has always been closely tied to the incompetent Wall Street investment banks that were not allowed to fail. They saw that she has tied herself to the college culture that says, "If you go to college, you get to do whatever you want, paid for by those who did not go to college." And they saw that she was a lawyer (a person who is often paid more than the producers of a product just to file paperwork). She was just another member of that privileged, non-productive class.

Of course they voted against her.

ADDING INSULT TO INJURY: IMMIGRATION AND THE PRIVILEGED CLASS

As if all of the above had not alienated the non-privileged classes enough, over the last years, Democrats have taken things further. With the Dream Act, children of illegal immigrants can now get government subsidies to attend college.

Many of the children of illegal immigrants who receive this aid (which they then immediately pass on to colleges through tuition) are also direct labor competition to the high school educated men. So first they have to send these children to college with their tax money, then the high school educated men have to compete with the same graduates for jobs.

At the same time, the privileged classes heavily block the immigration that could in any way compete with them. They do this primarily through restricting the total number of H1 visas (these are work visas for highly skilled labor). In fact, current proposals intend to keep the number of H1 visas lower than the number of refugee visas. The American Medical Association takes this even further, forcing any fully qualified foreign doctors to repeat their 4-5 year residencies in order to practice in the U.S. In other words, the privileged class does whatever it needs to do to remove any competition to itself. However, they allow competition to the unprivileged class, require the unprivileged class to pay for that competition, and also to pay for the intellectual hobbies of the privileged classes.

I'm not surprised they felt alienated. I'm impressed they have not gotten violent.

CONTINUING THE ECHO CHAMBER

Many Democrats have, at the very least, realized that something went wrong. But they are still using the closed off echo chamber to figure out what to do. Many discussion groups have been formed on Facebook and in the physical world to figure out what happened and what it means for the country as a whole. The one thing they are not doing though: inviting any non-Democrats. In fact, on the rare occasion a non-Democrat tries to contribute, he or she is invariably shut down.

After arrogance comes a fall. When you are so certain that everything you believe is right and everyone else is a moron, you make mistakes. That smug certainty, which is gradually giving way to psychological meltdowns, is preventing Democrats from getting the information they need in order to be effective.

If Democrats want to regain value dominance, they will have to learn to debate and listen again. They will have to learn to convert people, not just silence them. The new demand for authenticity cannot be ignored. Nor can the new skepticism found in a culture now swimming in information. The causes of Hillary's 2016 loss were not temporary aberrations, but fundamental changes to American politics. To succeed, future campaigns will have to adapt to this new political reality.

PERSONALITY POLITICS

THE SOURCE OF POLITICAL CORRECTNESS, AND THE UNSURPRISING BACKLASH

To many in the conservative movement, political correctness seems inexplicable. It seems that the world was pretty much normal, and then, all of a sudden, in the 1990s, every description became offensive. All kinds of politically correct terminology began appearing. Hyphenated Americans became the norm, even when factually false. For example, a black person was correctly referred to as an African American, even if that person was obviously British.

Sometimes, the new, politically correct terms presented as more pejorative than the original terms. Many people thought "little person" seemed ruder than "midget". This was made even more confusing when groups reappropriated words like "queer", previously considered a derogatory term.

People scrambled to try to remember the rapidly changing terms. New terms appeared every day, and are still appearing. Many people still to this day are afraid to tell stories involving their black friends, even if the story is humorous or uplifting, because no one really feels sure that they can avoid offense. In polite conversation, blacks are often referred to with highly nondescript descriptors instead. I have learned in politics that if someone is referring to "the guy wearing a suit" in a room in which everyone is wearing a suit, he is referring to the black guy.

The result of much of this scripted language has just been confusion and fear, and major impacts on people's level of comfort in conversing casually. Misusing or refusing to use a new PC term can have severe social and legal consequences, so it leaves people generally nervous. This issue has lead to protests, as when a Canadian professor recently refused to acknowledge multiple new genders, or use the gender neutral pronoun "ze", and of course has prompted several lawsuits.

When you speak with those who strongly believe in political correctness, you might expect to find extremely delicate people. But more often, you find people of high intelligence and iron resolve (that's an important clue).

Conservatives find the PC movement bewildering. Why have generations turned into such hypersensitive bubble people (immunologically-challenged Americans)?

Let me ask you this: when you are required to use politically correct speech, remodel your business to create politically correct bathrooms at your own expense, and give lip service to ideas you find maddening, how do you feel?

My guess: restricted, trapped, belittled, angered.

And recognizing the high intelligence and relent-less willpower of the minds behind PC culture, let's imagine that this did not just happen by accident. What would make someone want to make someone else feel restricted, trapped, belittled, and angered?

Obviously, being made to feel restricted, trapped, belittled, and angered themselves.

Consider the LGBTQ rights movement. For centuries, gays have received the worst kind of abuse. Even those who contributed massively to society were persecuted by government, and by the culture that controlled the government. Alan Turing, the father of modern computing, the man who helped crack the Nazi code and ensure Allied victory, was arrested and imprisoned, persecuted by the very nation he helped save. Why? Homosexuality. Eventually, he died young, almost certainly from the psychological, financial, and physical devastation caused by the above treatment.

And that's how they treated a national hero. How much worse was the treatment received by ordinary gay men and women? What about gays who could not access AIDS treatment, and ended up making their own knockoff medicines while they waited for FDA approval for drugs for some "gay disease"? Don't you think they knew that if it had been a disease striking married women, there would have been some kind of expedited access?

What about gays who were repeatedly told that marriage is between one man and one woman? These are people who had to hide themselves from society, who then worked up the courage to fight injustice and come out to friends and family. These people, despite all odds and social opposition, found someone whom they wanted to spend the rest of their lives with. And then they were told that the relationship that represented a lifetime of struggle was not real marriage. They were told that the union that they had fought ten times as hard as the average straight couple for did not count. It was not meaningful. That hard-earned triumph was not sacred. It was just immoral playacting.

What about blacks, who were blasted with fire hoses, had their civil rights stripped by Jim Crow laws, and were attacked by the government's literal police dogs? What about those who for much of history were enslaved, who have been targeted by drug legislation for decades, and who have received aggressive racial epithets for decades? Today there are more black men in prison than there were in slavery in 1850. All of this pressure on a person can incline them to push back.

Think about how often, even today, people are called derogatory words created to insult their sex, gender, race, and religious beliefs. Think about the decades and centuries of that resentment building up. Do you think it is any surprise that those who felt restricted and belittled will turn around and return the favor? Is it any surprise that those who received a lifetime of name calling will want to force people to call them by a particular name? And then add new names, pronouns, and rules to rub it in a bit? Is it surprising that those from Alan Turing's tradition might be tempted to force Christian bakers to bake them a cake? Or to force businesses to build new bathrooms?

I am not saying that it is right. Just that it is extremely understandable.

To correct this imbalance, marginalized groups worked through the Democratic Party in order to push their social values on the country. They worked to convince people in every way they could that equality was right, and people listened. These groups were heard, their plights taken seriously, and they gradually established value dominance over conservatives. They changed the face of this country. The right way became the liberal way, and people believed in liberal positions on social issues wholeheartedly enough to elect the first black president (twice) and legalize gay marriage nationwide. They finally achieved value dominance.

Upon achieving value dominance, the PC movement became both defensive and offensive. If everyone was struggling to remember the right thing to call people, they might have less time to come up with new derogatory words. If they were busy fighting laws about building new bathrooms, they might not have the energy leftover to be able to discriminate against trans people.

There is at least the appearance of people using Politically Correct culture as vengeance in recent years. A perfectly understandable vengeance, but vengeance nonetheless. Even if that is not the intent, it is certainly the perception.

In the past, conservatives have used laws and culture as weapons against minority groups. This pushed them toward political action. Conservatives managed to shut them up and make them hide, but could not stop them from organizing and voting. The conservative attempt to use legal and cultural force to secure their ideal societal rules paved the way for the complete loss of conservative value dominance. They refused to consider gay rights, or even basic decency. They were arrogant, dismissing the mere possibility of viewpoints counter to their own. After their arrogance came their fall.

Now, the tables have turned, and it is the liberals who are using laws and culture as weapons against conservatives. But this will only have the same result as before, degrading liberal views until they are no longer the dominant social belief system. In overusing their power after achieving value dominance, marginalized groups have been paving the way for their own defeat.

They have become just as arrogant and dismissive as conservatives were before. They called the movement "political correctness" not political politeness. They did not say, "this is a way to be courteous and considerate of others." They said, "if you do not do this you are wrong – ethically, socially, and legally."

All that arrogance has led to the start of the liberal fall from strength. Those who were on the receiving end of PC restrictiveness, who were silenced and forced to bear unexpected financial costs, were driven to the polls. The progressive movement's overuse of its hard gained value dominance pushed the election right into Trump's hands. Clinton's defeat was just as much a rejection of PC restrictiveness as it was of Clinton.

Progressives can regain value dominance. To do so, they have to use the methods that got them there in the first place. They will have to learn to debate and convince again, not just use social pressure to silence opposition. They will have to show themselves willing to at least listen to viewpoints other than their own.

RACISM

Unfortunately, Hillary supporters have listened even less since the election, and have shouted ever louder. Many have claimed that racism was the single biggest factor in the election. I'd like to offer a counter argument: Trump's aggressive rhetoric may have helped get the racist vote out a bit, but I can guarantee that Obama's skin color got the racist vote out a lot more.

As of now, the reports of racist outbreaks are unsettling, but they are not in large numbers, nor are they of new content. For example, some people have been chanting "Build That Wall." That's not new. They have been chanting that for years. I have heard "Build a Wall" chanted at all kinds of protests and rallies, including ones that have nothing at all to do with immigration. And people have been spray painting swastikas on walls for decades. There has been racially motivated violence for years. Political violence is less common, but most of the purely political violence has been directed at Trump supporters.

I strongly doubt that anything will ever get the racist vote out more than the first black president running for re-election. Trump's victory may have emboldened some racists a bit, and even a single loud racist in this context may make people nervous. There have been individual reports of violence against queer and trans people, but again, the numbers do not suggest a major increase caused by Trump's election. And it is always important to note that the media is not required to be non-discriminatory with the facts it presents, so an increase in reports of gay violence does not necessarily mean that gay violence was not horrific before, or that it has gotten incredibly worse in the past few weeks.

I believe this election was not really about race. The last two certainly were, given the racial differences between the candidates, but this one less so. So why does so much of this election seem to be about racism? Why is everyone talking about bigotry?

As it turns out, calling people racist is one of the most common techniques in politics. It is used all the time, by people on all sides of the political spectrum.

For example, those who want to end the War on Drugs often refer to it as "The Racist War on Drugs." There is an argument to be had that, at least in its application, the War on Drugs has been racially biased. Blacks are disproportionately targeted and historically have received harsher average sentences than whites for identical crimes. However, it is unlikely that all supporters of drug prohibition are racist. Many just think drugs are damaging and should thus be made illegal, and those who break the law should be jailed.

Those who oppose U.S. involvement in the Middle East are often called anti-Semitic. The argument is that U.S. military presence indirectly or directly supports Israel. However, it is unlikely that everyone who opposes a U.S. military presence in the Middle East is anti-Semitic. Many either oppose violence, or feel that there are no clear objectives or end point, or have other reasons for opposing U.S. military involvement in the Middle East.

For similar reasons, those who oppose foreign aid are often called, anti-Semitic, Islamophobic, xenophobic, and racist. After all, the U.S. gives foreign aid to Israel, plenty of Islamic countries, plenty of African countries, and plenty of Latin American countries. However, most opponents of foreign aid are motivated by financial interests, not racial ones.

Those who oppose public schooling are often called racist, as many minorities attend public school. However, most of them are motivated either by tax issues or educational quality issues, not White Supremacy.

Those who want to end programs like NAFTA are usually motivated by job concerns and financial concerns. However, NAFTA does involve Mexico, so opponents of NAFTA are often called anti-immigrant, anti-Hispanic, and racist.

The point is: labels like "bigot" or "racist" are often used for strategic and marketing reasons. That's not going to change any time soon. But it is vital to realize that it is not often, or even usually, particularly accurate. To find out what is really going on, it is necessary to look at other factors.

Take illegal immigration, for example. Those who oppose the Dream Act, which allowed children of illegal immigrants to receive taxpayer assistance for college tuition, were often called racist. After all, they were opposing the interests of primarily racial minorities.

However, having spoken to many opponents of that provision of the Dream Act and having read many articles and social media posts, it seems that the overwhelming opposition is actually to the financial cost. The Dream Act would cost more money. Those who voted against it would probably have also voted against giving tax money to descendants of the Mayflower crew as well.

Many who supported Trump opposed illegal immigration because employers routinely pay illegal immigrants below the state mandated minimum wage. Those who expect to be paid the minimum wage or higher are now put at a disadvantage. They have more competition. Those who work in career paths in which illegal immigrants form much of the labor supply obviously oppose illegal immigrants. If those illegal immigrants were not there, then the remaining Americans would have to be paid more. With a smaller supply of labor, wages would obviously rise. (Note: the economic reality is actually more complex than that, and often the presence of illegal immigrants can drive up the wages of Americans. After all, more laborers require more managers. But elections are rarely influenced by economic reality. They are influenced by economic perception. The current perception is that illegal immigrants are direct competition, and result in lower wages.)

By the way, doctors do the same thing. Right now, laws prevent successful, seasoned doctors from Britain,

Germany, Switzerland, Japan, and any other country from practicing medicine in the U.S. unless they redo their entire 4-5 year residency. Unfortunately, residencies for foreign doctors in America, particularly in competitive fields like orthopedic surgery or radiation oncology, are extremely difficult to secure. Even if doctors wanted to go through the process, it would be almost impossible.

This is not because doctors do not want "Red Coats and Japs tainting American Medicine with their filthy racial impurities." It is because doctors know that more competition will lower doctor wages. If there were ten times as many world class orthopedic surgeons in America as there are now, then their fees would be lowered through competition.

The AMA's opposition to allowing Oxford-trained physicians to practice medicine in the U.S. could be labeled "xenophobic." But we would recognize that label as missing the point. Doctors do not hate foreigners. They hate competition. So do people in every other field.

One of the particularly ludicrous arguments presented is that, "Illegal immigrants do the jobs that Americans do not want," and therefore allowing in more immigrants will not, in fact, increase competition.

To be frank, I make pretty high wages. But if you pay me double to pick apples instead, I'll be happy to do it. For that matter, if you pay me 10% more to pick apples instead, I'll do it.

It is not the jobs that Americans do not want. It is the lower wages. All people in all countries in the world prefer higher wages. In the labor market, that often comes by reducing your competition.

Trump got that. He knew that, with the exception of a very small percentage of the population, opposition to immigration was not about race. It was about money. For some, it was about lowering available competition in order to increase wages. For others, it was about not having to pay taxes for the health care, medical care, public schooling, or even food stamps for refugees and illegal immigrants.

Trump understood that while many people have all kinds of racial prejudices, those prejudices are much less important than financial concerns. Even people who are highly dedicated to particular beliefs routinely act contrary to those beliefs. Members of the KKK and other White Supremacy groups buy plenty of things that are made in China, entirely because they are cheaper. Sure, there are probably some diehards who do not, but those are the rare exception.

Those who decry the treatment of children in other countries often buy clothes made by children in other countries. Those who believe in raising livestock ethically often buy non-free-range chicken, because it is cheaper or the only option available.

It is not because people are lazy hypocrites. It is because everyone on earth has limited time and money.

Trump knew that it was about money. Hillary probably knew that too, but refused to acknowledge it in national addresses. This made those who opposed illegal immigration and refugee immigration for financial reasons feel dismissed and insulted. Because she refused to even acknowledge that there was any financial concern at all, she pushed away those who had any financial concern at all (basically everyone but millionaires and students who were still living off of their parents). In doing so, she pushed away huge portions of the populations that could have helped her win in a landslide.

WHAT THE ASIAN VOTE REVEALS

On a pure policy level, Asians have a lot to gain from a Democratic loss. The Democratic Party support many laws that disproportionately harm Asians.

For example, Asians are the most harmed by Affirmative Action in college admissions. In states where Affirmative Action is struck down, Asian students see huge increases in acceptance rates.

Furthermore, given the large percentage of high earners and business owners among Asians, they are disproportionately harmed by high taxes. It would make logical sense for them to overwhelmingly support anyone but the Democrats.

And yet, Asians vote overwhelmingly Democratic. And it is not because Asian parents do not care about college admissions. In fact, I do not think that anyone on earth cares more about anything than Asian parents care about college admissions.

So why do so many Asians vote Democratic, against their own pragmatic interests?

Having spoken to many Asian American voters (and being South Asian myself), I would say that most of it comes from feelings of marginalization and from perceived racism. Asians often believe that Republicans are racist

Let me give an example. Now that Trump has been elected and will have the opportunity to appoint Supreme court justices, it is likely that Affirmative Action will be struck down by the Supreme Court soon. This is great news for Asian Americans. In fact, I have had quite a few discussions with Asian American friends and family members over the last few days about this. Quite a few are pretty excited.

However, this excitement is nothing compared to the massive excitement from a year ago when Obama appeared on stage next to a Sikh American, and named a Sikh American to an advisory council on faith-based, neighborhood partnerships. Family and friemmnds were texting and emailing me. My Facebook feed was jammed with the same image.

Note that there was not any particular policy in that case. There was no tangible benefit to Asian Americans from this. However, they felt acknowledged; they had been given a seat at the table. They felt ignored and sidelined by Republicans. They felt respected by Democrats. That act of respect (and many others like it) are more than enough to compensate for the policies that pragmatically harm Asian Americans!

Democrats have used this brilliantly for decades, creating groups like "Progressive Hmong American Organizers." Obviously, this makes Hmong Americans feel included. Democratic strategists do not try to target parts of Hmong culture that are out of sync with current Western tradition. (For example, "Marriage by capture" is a practice in which the groom kidnaps the bride. In 1985, a Hmong man used a cultural defense to get out of a rape and kidnapping charge, since he argued he was practicing his cultural form of marriage.) Instead, Democrats make groups that may feel marginalized feel actively included.

This reveals an important strategic point. Sometimes you can win over a marginalized group just by offering them meaningless olive branches. It is not a question of policy, but a question of at least appearing to listen. In 2016, Trump understood this.

Trump saw that not all groups that feel marginalized are ethnic minorities. Some simply have political views outside the mainstream. Others have views that are secretly popular, but socially inappropriate to say out loud (e.g., opposition to PC culture).

Trump gave them a seat at the table. Even when he openly disagreed with them (for example, Trump has often spoken in favor of gay rights, a position with which some people do not agree), those voters did not feel ignored.

The important difference: Trump went after a numerically huge voting block (frustrated white men), rather than a comparatively small block (Asian Americans).

He also gave voice to their views. While Trump's anti-illegal-immigrant rhetoric was derided as racist, his audience understood the financial message it contained. When he talked about building a wall, they heard him giving them higher wages by reducing competition. While Democrats painted that as opposing all immigration and all minorities, those he was speaking to saw him reducing competition, increasing wages, and even reducing the taxes they would have to pay.

Trump understood that even pure racism is often just a twisted expression of frustration, and that the primary cause of that frustration is financial. He spoke their code. He understood their psychology. He spoke the language of money.

He did with this group of frustrated White men exactly what Democrats had done with Asians. It was not always about policy. It was about listening, expressing their views, and including them. The major difference: Trump's included groups were much, much bigger than Hillary's.

THE LATINO AND MUSLIM VOTES

Some exit polls suggested that Trump won 29% of the Latino vote; others suggest he got a record low 18%. Still, despite Trump's seemingly anti-Latino rhetoric, he got a far larger percentage than many Democrats ever would have predicted. In some parts of the country, like Florida, Trump got 31% of the Latino vote.

Many Democrats are shocked. How could even one percent of Latinos vote for someone who wants to deport them? How could anyone vote for someone who shows them that kind of disrespect?

To understand this phenomenon, you have to look at Trump's actual words – not at his opponent's summary of his words, or the media's summary of his words.

Trump wanted to deport illegal (undocumented) immigrants, not legal immigrants (who are the only ones casting votes). My guess is that makes him very, very unpopular among undocumented immigrants. But undocumented immigrants cannot vote or even legally donate to elections. So their views have zero impact on the election.

Most do not want to attract too much attention to themselves, so they do not apply much direct social pressure.

Plenty of social pressure was applied, on their
behalf, by voters in many camps. Democratic organizations who opposed Trump were obviously vocal, as were
Libertarians who tend to favor partially or entirely open
borders (although for most Libertarians, that goes along
with a simultaneous elimination of welfare).

Why didn't that work? Imagine this scenario.
Suppose a very wealthy white person from Orange County
moved to Monaco. Then, suppose Monaco had a referendum that would have the effect of allowing in large
numbers of poor, white homeless people from Los Angeles.

Monacans may assume that the rich person
from Orange county would strongly support such a
referendum. It is allowing in his people! His American
fellows. In fact, they are Americans who live only a few
miles away from his hometown.

Stereotypically, however, it is is unlikely that the
former Orange county resident would feel that way. Those
Americans are from a completely different social and
cultural class from him. He may view them as inclined to
poverty and violence, a drain on resources, and a threat to
safety. He might have even left to get away from them!

In addition, he realizes that as a white American,
he will now be judged by the behaviors of the white

homeless Americans from the same part of America as himself. People will make negative assumptions about him before they even meet him.

Most parts of the world have much, much greater class division than America. America has a comparatively large middle class; most other countries do not. Those who come to America legally often come from higher social classes in their home countries. Those who come illegally often come from lower social classes. Those of higher social classes do not place themselves in the same category as those in lower social classes, nor do they actively seek the company of these lower classes.

I know if I asked my Indian parents how they would feel about allowing large numbers of poor people from India into America, they would vitriolically oppose it. First, they would see them as a financial and tax liability. Second, they would see them as a threat to Indian American social status.

In America, Indian Americans enjoy a decently high social status, as most Indians who come here are doctors, engineers, or computer programmers, with of course quite a few stereotypical convenience store owners and taxi drivers. On the other hand, in the United Arab Emirates, Indians are seen as third class citizens because most Indians who go there are less educated, unskilled physical laborers.

Wealthy Latinos have absolutely nothing to gain, either socially or financially, from an influx of Latino laborers with lower education. In fact, at least socially, they might actually gain if undocumented workers were deported. If the stereotype of Latino shifted from laborer to engineer, it would increase their default social prestige.

Hillary's campaign forgot that Latin countries are just as differentiated as America, if not more so. While sometimes racially more homogeneous, Latin countries are even more economically differentiated.

The same, incidentally, holds true of Muslims. Many have been shocked to discover that three times as many Muslims voted for Trump as voted for Romney. According to the Council on American-Islamic Relations, 13 percent of Muslim voters voted for Trump, while only 4.4 percent voted for Romney. Given Trump's apparent anti-Muslim rhetoric, this seems inexplicable.

But racial minorities are used to dealing with prejudice. We are used to people making assumptions about us based entirely on how we look. The best we can do: change those assumptions. Thus, we prefer to make those assumptions as positive as possible.

While some Muslims have publicly argued for increasing the number of Syrian refugees, pretty much every American Muslim knows that Muslim refugees threaten their social perception. Yes, in a mosque you might discuss the importance of charity and brotherhood. But in private? If every other Muslim that people meet is an unskilled refugee with little cultural knowledge of the West? Obviously that will damage social perception of Muslims.

Muslims have always struggled for social acceptance in America, and never more than recently. Since 9/11, Muslims have seen their default social prestige plummet. Bringing in a large number of poor refugees would further hurt that overall social acceptance.

Every country has class divisions, and everybody cares about themselves more than the country they left. By ignoring class divisions present in source countries, Hillary's campaign overestimated its support among minority groups.

Immigrants can be both proud and sensitive, and politicians often make the mistake of being condescending. Here's an extreme example: suppose a politician is speaking to a group of Latinos, focusing on making sure that they have access to medical care and bilingual public education. If that group is mostly successful businessmen and doctors who put their kids in private schools, imagine how condescending and insulting the politician would seem! By the way, I have seen at least one local politicians make essentially the same mistake, by discussing access to welfare with a group of black people made up almost entirely of entrepreneurs.

To a lesser level, Hillary's campaign made that error. She did not in any way discuss the interests of successful legal immigrants (who can vote), and instead focused on the poorer undocumented immigrants (who cannot). Like many politicians, she assumed that targeting the needs of poor Latinos would automatically win over rich Latinos. But obviously, their goals are different. Her focus on making things better for illegal immigrants may have helped some suburban moms reduce "white guilt", but it did little to win over successful immigrants. And every cry of "racism!" against Trump further alienated many legal immigrants who supported what Trump said not for racial reasons but for social and economic ones.

LEADERSHIP

Before we approach the topic of sexism, it is vital to examine what leadership looks like. As an educator, I have the rare opportunity to observe groups of children naturally forming around leaders. I observe the attributes and behaviors, at an early age, that form the foundation for adult charisma.

In my role as a political strategist, I also get to see what that charisma looks like when expanded through experience.

With kids, you see some who are bossy and some who are leaders. You see this in both genders. You have bossy boys and bossy girls. You have leader boys and leader girls. The difference is this: leaders have a goal for the group, bossy people want to be in charge of the group.

For example, when you see leadership forming in a group of people who do not know each other, the leaders say, "Let's go get some pizza!" Or "Let's put a fish in the teacher's desk!" There is a goal of some kind that leaders use to rally people around. People naturally follow leaders because of their vision and fearlessness.

Bossy people, on the other hand, tend to fixate on wanting to be in charge. For example: "I'm the oldest, so I should be in charge." Even when people follow bossy people, they do so grudgingly.

In politics, leadership, or the illusion thereof, is vital. It is important to have a vision, or look like you have a vision. And it has to be a real vision. Not some phony sounding platitudes about children and the middle class, but a vision that is clear and specific. A vision connects to a very primal part of voters and advocates. Like children rallying around the one kid who has a silly plan, adults rally around those who have some kind of reasonable or inspiring or even ridiculous plan.

For Sanders, it was free college. Trump: the wall and deporting illegal immigrants. Ron Paul: End the Fed. Obama: government run healthcare.

Establishment candidates often forget how important this is. Romney's vision was...something about being nice? Israel might have been in there, or maybe the middle class. Possibly children.

Hillary's vision was...maybe something about the minimum wage, or America, or children. Maybe education?

Obviously, Hillary discussed policy in some long interviews, and on parts of her website. But she did not lead with that. She did not make any part of the election about her vision. She basically pointed out that she was not Trump, and that she was experienced.

Trump was like the kid saying, "Let's all wear red tomorrow, and confuse the teachers." Hillary was the kid saying, "I should be in charge, because I'm the oldest."

In many ways, Hillary came across the way Mitt Romney did in 2012. He showed no vision. Even when asked point blank what he would do, he only said, "I'm not gonna raise taxes." He did not talk about where he would go, but only talked about where he would not go. He was about children, Israel, the middle class, and not raising taxes. But he had no inspiring vision to rally supporters. In the eyes of most voters, he had no vision at all. His selling point was "not Obama", just as Hillary's was "not Trump".

Establishment candidates forget that they can also be populist candidates. All it takes is some kind of electrifying vision. In fact, Hillary had plenty to choose from. She could have adopted Sanders' free college. She could have focused on legalizing marijuana. There was no shortage.

Instead she fixated on being the first woman president ("I should be the president because I'm a woman!").

SEXISM

Just as it is quite easy to call someone a racist who may not, in fact, be one, it is also quite easy to call someone sexist. Those who oppose abortion are often called sexist. The hundreds of men and women I have discussed this topic with did not seem sexist. I doubt the millions of men and women who oppose abortion are all sexist.

Those who oppose paid maternity leave are sometimes called sexist. Most of those people also oppose paid paternity leave, so the label is probably not always accurate.

In insurance, young men generally pay more in car insurance than young women. However, in an open market, young women would pay more in health insurance than young men. The reason for the former: young men have historically been more prone to car accidents than young women. The reason for the latter: young women have historically been more prone to pregnancy than young men.

Those who believe in market based insurance rates, which would charge young women higher insurance premiums than young men, have been called sexist. But most of those are looking for financial fairness or simply lower costs for themselves, not expressing hatred for women.

In politics, sexism is as easy a charge to make as racism, but just as likely to be false.

Many of those who opposed Hillary Clinton supported Sarah Palin and Ann Coulter, and vice versa. It is possible that millions of people completely reversed their views on women in the last eight years. It is more likely that people just support people with whom they agree.

There are plenty of women leaders in the conservative movement and in the progressive movement. There are plenty of women who are Republican, Libertarian, Green Party, or independent elected officials, just as there are plenty of women who are Democratic elected officials.

Plenty of other countries have had women as presidents, prime ministers, chancellors, empresses, etc. England, Germany, India, and Argentina come to mind. It is not that these countries are particularly less sexist than the United States. In fact, some countries with female leaders are undoubtedly more so.

It is also important to note that Hillary likely received quite a few votes due to her gender. The "make history" narrative only made sense because she is a woman. In addition, more than half of the population is women. I talked to quite a few conservative women who indicated they strongly considered voting for her entirely based on her gender.

She certainly captured the majority of female voters (54%). But she did not even capture her closest demographic: the majority of white women (53%) voted for Trump.

She did completely fail to capture male voters. Hillary captured 41% of the male vote. That's a gender gap of 13 percent, the highest in history. But not much higher than the 12% gender gap that Al Gore had in 2000. And the closeness of the two gender gaps reveals something important.

COOLNESS AND POLITICS

Al Gore was debilitatingly uncool. He lacked vision of any kind, and he spoke primarily in tedious platitudes. He bragged about coining the term "information super-highway", possibly the least cool term ever used to describe the internet. He seemed unable to challenge any part of the status quo. Much like this election, the 2000 election was a close race to the bottom. People thought Bush was a moron. People thought Gore was boring and tedious. Gore was just better at losing than Bush.

Hillary Clinton had a similar problem. Her speeches were one tedious platitude after another. She had no vision. She seemed unable to challenge any part of the status quo, or even enforce it interestingly. The only thing interesting about her was her gender.

She had no anti-establishment credentials of any kind, and refused even the easy ones handed to her (like legalizing marijuana). She did not even have an interesting pro-status quo stance, as Reagan did with his "moral majority" focus.

She lacked charisma. Charisma comes from fearlessness connected to a vision or unusual view. Trump had plenty of charisma.

She lacked charm, which comes from making the listener feel comfortable, listened to, and cared about. Bill Clinton had plenty of charm. Even those who disagreed with him did not feel dismissed by him.

What's interesting is that as First Lady, she actually started to develop a kind of charisma. Sure, it was rough around the edges and abrasive, but it could have been a starting point. Many charismatic people start off a bit abrasive, and then learn how to walk the line between charismatic and rude. They also know that if occasionally they step over the line, it is no huge deal. Trump steps over the line shamelessly; it only adds to his charisma.

With practice and polish, she could have developed that initial spark of charisma into something socially and politically more effective. But instead she chose to play it safe, take no interesting positions, make no waves. In the senate, she pretty much constantly supported the status quo. While Obama spoke out against the war in

Iraq, demonstrating vision and courage, she gave the most equivocating speech in the history of speeches, and then tentatively, with great conviction, decided to support the war. Here are a few quotes:

"I also greatly respect the differing opinions within this body. The debate they engender will aid our search for a wise, effective policy. Therefore, on no account should dissent be discouraged or disparaged."

This tangled language does nothing but state the blatantly obvious. Hillary begins with the platitude that people in the Senate sometimes disagree and that debate is good. She then points out that disagreements in the U.S. Senate should not be silenced (silencing disagreements in the Senate, of course, is not a realistic possibility).

"If we were to attack Iraq now, alone or with few allies, it would set a precedent that could come back to haunt us... Others argue that we should work through the United Nations and should only resort to force if and when the United Nations Security Council approves it...But there are problems with this approach as well... While there is no perfect approach to this thorny dilemma, and while people of good faith and high intelligence can reach diametrically opposed conclusions, I believe the best course is to go to the UN for a strong resolution that scraps the 1998 restrictions on inspections and calls for complete, unlimited inspections with cooperation expected and demanded from Iraq." After hundreds of words of beating around the bush, reiterating how much she "respects" everyone, and spelling out how challenging the situation is, she more or less gets to some kind of recommendation that is barely decipherable from her explanation of it.

Since many readers may not have read that boringness, she is basically speaking in favor of unilateral inspections and de facto war powers for the president. The obvious effect would have been that Iraq would have refused, leading to war.

Obama, on the other hand, was fearless and charismatic to the point of rude:

"What I am opposed to is a dumb war. What I am opposed to is a rash war....I also know that Saddam poses no imminent and direct threat to the United States or to his neighbors, that the Iraqi economy is in shambles, that the Iraqi military a fraction of its former strength, and that in concert with the international community he can be contained until, in the way of all petty dictators, he falls away into the dustbin of history. I know that even a successful war against Iraq will require a U.S. occupation of undetermined length, at undetermined cost, with undetermined consequences."

Obama, Bill Clinton, Sanders, and Trump were cool. Hillary Clinton and Al Gore were not.

Some people think that Hillary's lack of social coolness can be attributed to a defect in social education given to women. They argue that men are taught some things that women are not.

It has been argued that women are taught not to challenge authority or the status quo, while men are taught the opposite. Women are taught never to "swim upstream". Men are always, without question, to fight against all odds.

But Hillary has been swimming upstream her entire life. She seems to have figured that part out. Unfortunately, she has not demonstrated an understanding that leadership is not just about promoting yourself, and courage is not just supporting the most popular view. This is not some secret known only to men. The real issue is not sexism, but lack of skill in the areas that matter to voters.

People often think that those who are anti-establishment (against the current) are cooler than those who are part of the establishment. We admire people like William Wallace in *Braveheart*, or Martin Luther King in real life, who both faced huge odds without giving up. We respect people like that far more than we admire those who climb to the top of some bureaucratic ladder.

Thus, when someone is bossy instead of visionary, ladder climbing instead of fearless, word-mincing instead of direct, we despise them a bit, regardless of gender.

One of the most famous quotes on the renegade type of courage comes from a book written by a woman, where the protagonist is a young girl, and the example of courage is an old woman. Here's the quote, from Harper Lee's To Kill a Mockingbird:

"I wanted you to see what real courage is, instead of getting the idea that courage is a man with a gun in his hand. It is when you know you're licked before you begin but you begin anyway and you see it through no matter what. You rarely win, but sometimes you do."

The idea that women are somehow ignorant of the true nature of courage is preposterous. Clearly, people of all genders know that courage is standing up for what's right, against all odds. And people respect those who do just that. They also reject anyone who maintains the status quo and pretends that she is truly courageous just because of her gender.

Hillary does not project the kind of renegade, cool abrasiveness that voters view as real courage.

On the other side, Trump practically epitomizes those qualities. Trump, in his own aggressive, unapologetic, authentic, crude way is highly charismatic. He's real, raw, and funny, like an R-rated comedian. Hillary is as fun as a bossy hall monitor, and as phony as political promises.

Abrasiveness works when combined with authenticity. That's the secret of many great offensive comedians. But when abrasiveness is combined with phoniness you get an unacceptable combination. Phoniness has to be combined with relentless charm. Ronald Reagan and Bill Clinton knew that. Despite both being liars, they were both popular and are still well liked.

Both knew how to show down to earth humility, even if it was faked. But Hillary just did not get that. For example, when Hillary said on election day that it was "humbling to vote for herself," millions of Americans found themselves thinking, "Wow. She really does not know what humility is at all." Every time she said, "humbling", millions of Americans thought, "You keep using that word. I do not think it means what you think it means."

COOLNESS, NOT SEXISM

It should be noted that Hillary's personality would be just as unforgivable in a man. If anything, she may have been given more leeway because she is a women. You do not see many men succeed in politics who are simultaneously arrogant, pro-establishment, abrasive, phony, dismissive, word mincing, prissy, and equivocating. It would be too devastating a combination. That kind of a man simply could not survive the jungle of politics, or of anything else.

If anything, that leeway damaged her. Had Democrats refused to make allowances for her because she was a woman, had they held her to the same

WHY HILLARY LOST   111

standards of personality to which they held other
Democrats, she could have grown into a more charismatic
and charming person over the last 20 years.

But instead, she became increasingly unlikable.
Even when Oprah Winfrey publicly endorsed her, Winfrey
said, "She's not coming over to your house! You don't have
to like her. You don't have to like her."

But that was the problem. Her unlikability, her
persona of a ladder climber instead of a leader, her lack
of any anti establishment credibility, her perceived lack
of courage, and her image as a corporate shill was all too
much. That level of unlikability and national politics
just do not mix. No matter how much money, how much
name recognition, and how many political connections
you have, when so many people despise your personality,
it just does not work.

POPULAR VS. UNPOPULAR POLICY

Coolness and likeability are not confined to personality;
politicians can win or lose campaigns based on the
popularity of the policies they choose to support.

In any political party, there are policies that are
popular within the party, and policies that are popular to
potential converts. Within the Libertarian Party, ending the
Federal Reserve and switching to a gold backed currency

is popular. However, it is not a great way to start outreach to most voters. When I am doing outreach, I might start with ending the War on Drugs, ending Foreign Wars, or ending Common Core. These ideas have traction with huge percentages of Americans. It is important to know whether you are preaching to the choir or engaging in missionary work.

Republicans and Democrats also have policies that are popular, and useful for outreach. The vast majority of Americans are pro-choice and favor marijuana legalization. These can be useful tools for Democratic Party outreach. Most people want lower taxes and an end to Common Core. Those are good outreach tools for Republicans.

The Republican and Democratic parties have secondary concerns because of the large donations they receive and the high costs of their campaigns. There are some issues that are popular with voters, other issues are popular with the largest donors. It is a tough balancing act.

For example, war is highly unpopular with voters. On the other hand, it is highly popular with defense contractors who profit from military expenditure. Thus, candidates have to choose between the message that is popular with voters and a message popular with those who fund their advertising.

Outside of the Democratic Party, Affirmative Action is highly unpopular. Inside the Democratic Party, it is pretty popular. A candidate who wants to do outreach would focus on issues popular outside their party. A candidate who wants to mobilize the base and get the vote out would focus on issues popular within the party.

The Clinton campaign made the mistake of dismissing non-Democratic voters. They appealed to the financial supporters of the campaign instead. Hillary presented policy positions that were favored by Wall Street and Defense Contractors, two vital donor bases. She also presented policy positions that were favored by the Democratic base.

However, she did not present any policies favored by voters outside of those two groups. She certainly could have. At this point, marijuana legalization is basically inevitable. When asked directly, she could have supported facilitating research on marijuana's medical benefits. But she did not take the easy opportunity to support marijuana legalization. Had she done so, she could probably have drawn many more independent and even Libertarian voters. Instead, she ignored almost all non-Democrats, giving them no reason to vote for her. Her primary argument was that she was not Trump. It was not enough.

There is a difference between leadership and ladder climbing. There is a major difference between persuasion and pandering.

During the campaign, Clinton showed that she was ambitious. And she made plenty of politician-esque statements about children and the middle class. But she showed no vision. She never tried to persuade anyone of anything other than "Vote for me," or perhaps, "Trump is bad."

Trump and Sanders, however, both spent time trying to persuade people of particular policy positions. They happen to be policies that I do not personally agree with, but fighting for those ideas portrayed them as leaders, not ladder climbers or panderers. Bernie Sanders argued that college should be paid for by taxes, and that no student should have college debt. Trump argued in favor of building a wall. Having a vision, even a wrongheaded one, separates leaders from ladder climbers.

Interestingly enough, in the past, even as first lady, Hillary showed plenty of vision. She argued hard to persuade people for the need for socialized medicine and healthcare reform. While I disagree personally, that argument showed leadership. By choosing to be "moderate" instead of persuasive, her campaign obviously failed to persuade anyone. By focusing on not-losing instead of winning, she did not gain any converts.

Sanders brought new voters into the Democratic Party. Trump brought new voters into the Republican Party. Even Johnson brought new voters into the Libertarian Party, and Stein to the Green Party. But Hillary did not bring new voters into the Democratic party, with the possible exception of 18-year-olds who had already planned to vote Democratic.

In fact, Hillary received 6 million fewer votes than Obama in 2012; she lost millions of the voters that Obama had brought into the party. The key point here is: this was not just a failure of outreach. Hillary also failed to retain her own voter base. She lost young voters who responded to Obama's authenticity. She drove away the antiwar left who supported Obama in 2008 with her hawkish policy stances. She drove away the pro-legalization bloc that had supported Obama. If she had managed to retain those voters, she would have easily won.

This failure may affect the balance of power for the next 2-4 years. Without the standard presidential election year boost, the Democrats will need to find new ways to grow their numbers.

BEING A GOOD PERSON

Personality politics has been an issue for more than just this election. One of the constantly mocked behaviors of Democratic voters is that once Obama was elected, they stopped protesting the same war they had protested while Bush was in power.

At first glance, it seems hypocritical, immoral, or just plain stupid. If a war is worthy of protesting under Bush, wouldn't the identical war be worth protesting under Obama?

During the last eight years, I have asked many, many Democrats about this. And it roughly comes down to this: they considered Bush to be dishonest, untrustworthy, and a bad person. They considered Obama to be honest, trustworthy, and a good person. They trusted him fundamentally, so they trusted his judgement. If he said we needed to be in Afghanistan, then we needed to be in Afghanistan.

The Democratic leadership knows all this, and has spent a lot of time promoting the idea that Obama is a good, decent guy. Even after the election, an explosively viral video depicts his friendship with Joe Biden. It is lighthearted and sweet. A related series of image memes, showing the playful and friendly relationship between the president and the vice president have circulated. Even some Libertarians and Republicans have shared the images due to the humor and pleasantness in them. Much of Democratic social media outreach includes things like reminding people when it is Obama's birthday, or the birthday of a member of the first family.

Interestingly, my progressive friends often like to tell me personal details about politicians that they like. My conservative friends usually focus on particular policies.

It is not that policy does not matter to those Democrats. It is that trust matters more.

Among many Democrats, being a good person is the most important thing – not only for politicians, but for themselves. It is a goal in life.

In fact, being a good person is often more important than being a skilled person.

Take the response of Daniel Tammet, author of *Born on a Blue Day*, to a famous quote from the show the West Wing. The West Wing, a Democratic leaning show, has one of the characters respond to the idea that the rich do not pay their fair share:

"I left Gage Whitney making $400,000 a year, which means I paid 27 times the national average in income tax. I paid my fair share, and the fair share of 26 other people. And I'm happy to, 'cause that's the only way it's gonna work. And it's in my best interest that everybody be able to go to schools and drive on roads. But I don't get 27 votes on Election Day. The fire department doesn't come to my house 27 times faster and the water does not come out of my faucet 27 times hotter. The top one percent of wage earners in this country pay for 22 percent of this country. Let's not call them names while they're doing it, is all I'm saying."

What's interesting is the response to such a comment by Tammet:

"Sam, you paid more than 20 times the national average in income tax because you were being paid more than 20 times the national average in income. You're not 20 times a better person than the average man."

From an economic standpoint, the fictional character was 27 times more valuable, that's why he was paid that much more. But that's not Tammet's point. He is not 27 times more decent, trustworthy, and nice. He's not 27 times more empathetic, not 27 times more honest, not 27 times more trustworthy, or 27 times more kind.

TRUSTWORTHINESS AND DECENTNESS

Trustworthiness and decentness have been extremely important to many Democratic voters for decades.

That was the secret behind Bernie Sanders' success. Many voters trusted him. Even those who did not agree with his policies still voted for him in the primary. As a relative outsider, he should not have stood a chance against Hillary. But his campaign went far.

The same applied to Obama, especially in 2008. He understood the idea of authenticity. But Hillary has always come across as an arrogant phony. Thus, while Hillary's policies in 2008 were around the same level of popularity as Obama's, she did not have the authenticity to gain trust.

As a simple example: during the 2008 primary debate, Obama and Hillary were asked what their biggest weaknesses were. Obama said "messy desk". Hillary said, "I am just too impatient to bring about change in America."

Not realizing she had clearly lost the vital authenticity battle, Hillary's campaign pushed hard, insinuating that someone with a messy desk was not fit to be president. Obama's response: "If I had gone last, I would have known what the game was. I could have said, 'Well ya know, I like to help old ladies across the street. Sometimes they don't want to be helped. It's terrible.'"

The crowd laughed at Obama's mockery of Hillary's phony answers. And their trust in Obama grew.

When asked if he smoked marijuana and if he inhaled, Obama said, "Yes, I inhaled. That was the whole point." He understood a generation that valued realness and authenticity.

In fact, in 2008, even I voted for Obama. It was the first (and only) time I ever voted for a non-Libertarian for president.

Trust is absolutely vital to the success of any Democratic contender. Trump knew that. That's why he constantly called her "Crooked Hillary" instead of "Tax and Waste Hillary." He knew that Democratic voters would not be swayed by policy. If they trust a person, they will support a policy that they otherwise would not support if an untrustworthy person suggested it. After all, they protested Bush's war but accepted Obama's identical war.

Hillary's campaign never got that. They had every opportunity for authenticity in the campaign. They could have made fun of FBI Director Comey or mocked Trump's constant antics. If Hillary did not feel comfortable doing so herself, she could have had Kaine do it for her. After all, it is often the Vice Presidential candidate's job to be the aggressive one, while the president presents a more polished, calm position.

But she did not do that. Instead, she presented a tedious, "professional", phony, and inauthentic appearance. She seemed interested in climbing the ladder, but not interested in anyone but herself. All that may be false. She may be a genuinely caring and philanthropic person, but that's not how she came across.

It was even in her campaign slogan: "I'm with Her." Her slogan was not about the people. It was about the people helping her. Compare that to Obama's message: Hope. It was not about his hopes. It was about the hopes of the electorate. Or to Trump's slogan: "Make America Great Again." A clunkier slogan, but one that was still about the people.

Democrats have, in the past, seemed to understand personality politics. They just need to remember this lesson during the next primaries if they want to give their values the best chance at winning in 2020.

NOT RUNNING FOR SAINT

For many voters, it is important that their president represent traditional family values. They want someone who has never been divorced, never cheated on a spouse, never done anything bad.

The problem: neither Hillary nor Trump fit that mold. Trump has been divorced often; he's a routine guest on Howard Stern's show, and he's an incorrigible womanizer. His current wife is only 11 years older than his daughter. Hillary was involved in a marriage in which she explicitly or implicitly accepted her husband's womanizing. Neither really represented old fashioned family values.

That battle had been lost by both, but only Trump accepted it. Within days of the his most unsavory comment, caught on tape, the slogan "He's not running for saint" became a political buzz-phrase heard everywhere.

But Hillary kept running for saint, continuing to present a holier-than-thou attitude. It only worked among her strongest supporters, who already worshipped her. With many other voters, it was a huge turnoff. Any casual observer could see that she had lived as compromised a life as anyone, bent the rules as much as anyone, if not more. Her marriage seemed a political facade, her Wall Street connections a clear example of blatant greed, if not corruption.

It is not inherently a big deal. Most of us do not have perfect relationships or marriages. Many of us do things to make more money. We do whatever we can to pay lower taxes, to get out of speeding tickets, etc.

Trump owned it. When challenged on not paying taxes, he just said, "That makes me smart."

Hillary did not get it. She kept hammering that point, while denying her own arguably more corrupt greed. She insisted that we playact with her, and pretend that there has been a single person in the history of ever that does not try to pay the lowest taxes possible. This made her seem like some super out of touch second grade teacher, saying, "You should love to share," instead of the cool teacher saying, "Yeah, sharing is annoying, but if you don't do it you look like a social outcast."

My guess: Trump intentionally manipulated her into it. If he had actually not wanted to show his tax returns, he just would not have. But instead, he tricked her campaign into putting its own effort and outreach into focusing on his tax returns. He let it drag on for months, building up suspense. He does know a bit about reality TV after all. Then he let Hillary damage herself with her own words. She tried to hammer him for doing everything legally possible to pay lower taxes.

In the privacy of their own minds, 99.999% of Americans thought, "You know who else tries to pay lower taxes? Me."

Every time she attacked that, she looked phonier and phonier. The time and energy she wasted on these attacks just made her look increasingly inauthentic and out of touch. Instead, she could have been attacking Trump's policies or promoting her own, making real political gains. She just did not understand the actual mindset of the country.

Going forward, it seems worthwhile for Democrats to remember that Americans demand realism and authenticity, not the sanctimonious facades that were in fashion decades ago. Society has changed in a crucial way, and Democrats need to catch up with this fact.

By the way, this was not the first time Trump had used the free publicity technique. Throughout most of the Republican primary he did that. He'd say something offensive, and let the media cover and attack him, thus making his issues the center of the primary. He rode one free publicity wave after another, working the media like an instrument.

THE SOCIAL IGNORANCE OF THE MEDIA

As if Hillary's dismissiveness and ignorance about personality politics were not enough, the media joined in to help secure Trump's victory.

Imagine this: in late elementary school, students often start to reproduce the off color humor they have absorbed from television, older peers, and elsewhere. The jokes are usually funny, but highly inappropriate, as elementary schoolers are wont to push the boundaries of their social limitations as they explore their own personalities and the world around them.

So you have young students telling jokes, other students laughing uproariously, and a teacher claiming bitterly that she cannot even see how such a joke could begin to be funny.

As adults, we know the teacher is trying to stop students from being crude or mocking. But the students telling the jokes see the teacher as an uncool, socially oblivious overlord who would have them limit themselves to observational humor and knock-knock jokes.

Pretending something hilarious is not funny never makes a person seem cool, it makes him or her seem socially blind and out of touch with reality.

Take the following exchange, for example:

Clinton: "It is just awfully good that someone with the temperament of Donald Trump is not in charge of the law of our country"

Trump: "Because you'd be in jail."

This joke came across as a well-timed zinger. It was a clever, funny insult, and it clearly was viewed by audiences as a quip about Clinton's email scandals and their potential illegality. Millions watching laughed, and many commentators considered it a strong moment for Trump.

Quickly, however, the press turned into everyone's least favorite elementary school overlord. *Slate.com* ran an article with the subheading: "By threatening to jail his opponent, Donald Trump promised to rip up the foundations of liberal democracy."

At no point does the article consider either that Trump was just delivering a humorous insult, or that Trump simply meant he would make sure no unfair exceptions were made for the politically powerful.

Even Republicans joined in. Stuart Stevens, campaign manager for Mitt Romney, tweeted, "Only time I have ever heard a candidate threatening to jail his opponent was in the Congo. He lost & was later convicted of war crimes."

The problem was that those watching or listening to the debate knew that such analysis was far from accurate. Trump was mocking an opponent's corruption, not threatening to hold her in Guantanamo without trial. Much of the media lost credibility with many voters.

If media outlets had said that the joke was in poor taste, they would have looked like the teacher who does not want you to have any fun, but at least they would not have looked like total idiots. They might have even managed to convert a few people who do not approve of crude or attacking humor. But instead, in an attempt to demonize Trump they chose to intentionally misinterpret his comments. They lost that battle.

Those who either do not like or do not get attack humor generally seem out of touch. They do not seem cool or socially intelligent. Trump, for the most part, got humor. Throughout the 2016 campaign, Trump made aggressive and shameless jokes. A few were boorish and showed a lack of social skills. Most others were funny and intelligent.

The media got in the habit of attacking Trump for saying moronic things. In fairness, he gave them plenty to work with. For example, when a soldier gave Trump his own Purple Heart medal, Trump said that he "always wanted to get the Purple Heart." This was a bit stupid, since a Purple Heart medal is given to a soldier who is wounded or killed in the line of duty.

When he mocked the parents of a Muslim soldier, that was a bit tasteless. When he mocked a disabled reporter (which he denies, but the video does not look good), that was also a bit foolish.

The media attacked that behavior, which makes sense. Attacking Trump when he's being socially inept is perfectly reasonable. Later, however, the media started attacking Trump in ways that made the media seem out of touch, socially inept, and prone to exaggeration.

In July, 2016. In a press conference, Trump said, "Russia, if you're listening, I hope you're able to find the 30,000 emails that are missing." This was an obvious mocking of Clinton's email server issue, and the fact that some of it may have been covered up.

Once again, the media decided to go with the social obliviousness strategy. *The Washington Post* ran a headline that said, "Trump invites Russia to meddle in the U.S. presidential race with Clinton's emails."

This kind of deliberate misinterpretation and exaggeration of what was obviously a joking insult destroyed the reputation of the media for many voters. Voters could see the speech live, on video. In fact, the video clips were linked in the article. Just because the media pretended not to get the jokes did not stop people from watching and laughing.

Democratic supporters who tried to push the media narrative on these issues only made themselves look either biased or obtuse. On social media, I got several messages about Trump inviting Russia to meddle in American elections, and saw hundreds of posts and tweets. It was the wrong fight for Democrats to pick. It just made them look bad.

They should have just said that the comments were in poor taste, and then focused on the many other socially questionable statements Trump had made. There was no shortage to choose from. Instead, they diluted that message by including funny attacks by Trump, actually spreading some of Trump's better moments to those who had not seen them, and making themselves look stupid. It was a bad strategy.

TIRED OF MORONS

The American populace is tired of authority figures misinterpreting things moronically. In 2014, when a 10 year old boy in Florida was suspended for making a gun shape with his fingers, it struck many people as preposterous. In 2015, a fourth grader was suspended for threatening to make another student vanish with his magical ring (inspired by the *Lord of the Rings*). Most people considered that decision silly. When, in 2013, a 6 year old boy was suspended for sexual harassment for kissing a girl on the hand, many considered it absurd. Many Americans are tired of things being interpreted in exaggerated, out of context ways.

When a school system does that, it looks like a moronic bureaucracy. When a reporter does that, he just looks like a moron.

But it may point to a deeper issue. Trump has brought a new level of brazen authenticity to politics. He says what he wants, and does not follow the rules of political speaking. Before politics, he talked about all

kinds of things as a guest on Howard Stern's show, and
in plenty of other places. He did not feel the need to
apologize for his personal behavior.

The important question is: can American political
journalism handle that? Can they report on people who
refuse to use polispeak, who refuse to apologize for
common behavior even if priests might not like it? Are they
able to live in a world in which a President saying "pussy" in
private but on tape does not end his political career?

Because that world is here. Empty platitudes
about children and the middle class can no longer be the
substance of American political discourse. While plenty
of presidents have been womanizers, in Trump we see
someone who is unapologetically so. American journalism
needs to adjust to that. For most of American history an
extramarital affair could be the end of a political career, but
clearly that is no longer the case.

As the old saccharine veneer of politics chips
off, will the media be able to adjust? Or will they keep
reporting on minor scandals long after anyone finds
them scandalous? Will they be able to compare the
statements of politicians to normal speech, rather than
political speech? Will they realize that the old America,
which would have been scandalized if a First Lady wore
white after labor day, is now gone?

In its November 13, 2016 letter to its readers, the *New York Times* asks, "Did Donald Trump's sheer unconventionality lead us and other news outlets to underestimate his support among American voters?" The answer: obviously. And if they continue to pretend Americans are the saps they once were, instead of the skeptics they now are, they will continue to misjudge American politics.

We are no longer living in overly polite delusions of politics. *West Wing* has now given way to *House of Cards*. The old politics is over, and with it, the old style of political reporting is obsolete.

LOCKER ROOM TALK

Our discussion of the media brings us to one of the most pressing questions of the 2016 election: Why didn't "Grab them by the pussy" destroy Trump's chance of victory? When the entire country heard Trump apparently boast about sexual assault, why didn't that end it? How did he win after that?

This section, because of its subject matter, will explore offensive language. In order to understand the significance of Trump's statement and the political strategy implications, we must examine frankly and directly the substance of inappropriate conversations common in America.

The media's failure to honestly engage in this type of analysis lead to their massively wrong predictions on the outcome. A sugar coated analysis cannot accurately analyze the real underbelly of common conversation.

At the time, many, including me, saw the release of the "Trump Tapes" as the turning point of the election. Before the Trump Tapes, many thought that Trump had a solid chance. Social media certainly seemed to indicate that. When Trump posted on Facebook, thousands of adoring fans cheered him on. When Hillary posted on Facebook, thousands insulted and derided her.

But after the tapes, many political experts saw his cause as hopeless. Even the Republican establishment started to withdraw support. Republican senators, governors, and congressmen withdrew their endorsement. Paul Ryan cancelled a joint appearance. RNC Chair Reince Priebus looked like a man who just found out he had 6 hours to live.

Politicians only pull endorsements like that when they believe a cause is completely hopeless. After all, in a world of political favors, no one wants to end up on the wrong side of a president!

The Clinton campaign shifted focus from winning the presidency to winning the Senate. They assumed, like everyone else, that there was no possible chance that Trump could win the presidency.

But everyone was wrong. Somehow, the tapes did not matter.

During the chaos, there were arguments presented on both sides. In Trump's favor, it was a private conversation, not a political speech. But in some ways, that made it worse. In those tapes, we were not seeing the entertainer who we suspected was being offensive on purpose in his public persona. This was not just someone trying to get free media attention by saying something offensive, as Trump had repeatedly done throughout the primary.

This was Trump the man. These words seemed to reveal his true self.

On the other hand, Trump supporters dismissed it as "locker room talk." They argued that people intentionally said crass things in private, and that such comments were neither uncommon nor meaningful.

Clinton supporters insisted that it was inappropriate in any setting. One actor after another claimed that they had never heard such talk, even inside a locker room.

For political strategy, the critical question here is not, "Is that a good thing to say." We can safely agree that there is not much of a positive in bragging about grabbing women by the privates without invitation. The real questions, from the standpoints of political strategy, are:

1. How common is this type of language?
2. How severe was this particular example?

The first question asks, generally, how common is this type of aggressively crude sexual language. The second question asks, how comparatively crude was Trump's statement compared to other crude language? On a scale of 1 to 10, how crude is it?

Actors and the news media suggested that this type of language is rare even in private. They claimed that even privacy was no excuse for this type of language; this comment would rate a 10 on the crudeness scale. Now obviously, a nice guy actor will pretend to be a nice guy. That is literally his job. But the Clinton campaign and many Democrats seemed to be convinced by these "nice guy" characters, and fully believed that such a comment would destroy Trump's chances.

Even the Republicans seemed to agree.

But was it really so rare? Was Trump's language so unusually offensive as to wreak so much havoc?

PART 1: TRUMP VS. PUBLIC ENTERTAINMENT

Before I compare Trump's words to actual locker room conversations, let's see how they compare to public conversations. After all, private locker room conversations are often cruder than what we see in public entertainment and social gatherings.

Public discourse in today's America is different than what it was fifty years ago. Humor is raunchier, descriptions are more explicit, content is far more violent. This may not be good, but it is definitely true.

Rap songs on the radio routinely have barely hidden sexual lyrics. A decade or so ago, phrases like "skeet, skeet, skeet" often formed the background of songs. Before that, the song "Candy Shop", a song entirely about oral sex, was quite popular among many elementary schoolers. A schoolteacher acquaintance bemoaned the fact that her fifth graders loved to loudly sing it on the bus (and yes, they knew what the lyrics meant).

You can find worse in 90s alternative rock. Stone Temple Pilots' *Sex Type Thing* is an unsettling song from the perspective of a rapist. It went all the way up to #23 on the U.S. Album Rock Tracks chart.

Video games go further. The most famous is the *Grand Theft Auto* series. One of the primary ways to get money in the game (which you use to buy weapons, etc.) is to beat up and rob scantily-clad prostitutes. This series is one of the most popular darkly comedic games in the world.

Nor is this just for men. Comedian Allie Wong has joked about anally devirginizing as many men as she could, helping them find their male g-spot.

The main character "Chanel" (Emma Roberts) in the show *Scream Queens*, which comedically portrays a sorority facing a serial killer, routinely refers to her underlings as "gashes" (crass slang for vagina) and "idiot hookers." She suggests that a pledge wearing a neck brace for scoliosis "probably sprained her neck giving blumpkins down at the local bowling alley."

Political comedies are not much different. The political comedy *Veep* is known for its shameless humor. One character indicates about the protagonist, "She's changed her mind more times than a fricking child molester in Disneyland." Another character describes a congressional strategy like this: "Once you're all done with them, I'll move in and squirt a half gallon of ropey jism into their mottled congressional cornholes." Even the female protagonist (played by Julia Louis-Dreyfus) is known for her vulgar statements, such as "He knows I've got a bigger role in the White House now, which means I've got a bigger dick, which means he can suck it."

Take all that into account: big shows designed for the public, with big budgets, writing teams, legal teams, and heavy marketing. This is not private, crass joking. It is not accidentally leaked tapes. This is all intentional, aggressively promoted content.

Even parlor games are following suit. Look at the explosively popular game "Cards Against Humanity", in which players try to connect the most inappropriate and crass answers to given questions. For example: "What brought the orgy to a grinding halt?" Popular Answer on the Internet: "Child Protective Services." Or "If God didn't want us to enjoy _____, he wouldn't have given us _____." Popular Answer on the Internet: "Ethnic Cleansing...Brown People."

Even open supporters of Hillary Clinton, such as the writer of my favorite nerd comic XKCD, have no problem with inappropriate humor. In one comic strip, he lists possible baby names for a daughter. One of the many intentionally preposterous names was Astamouth.

Compared to what is common on the radio, on TV, and even in parlor games, Trump's private boasting is about middle of the road. His intentionally crass private boasting is about average for public entertainment standards.

That may not be a good situation. America as a whole may be better off with a more genteel style of communication. But the simple fact is that even by public standards, Trump's private jokes were nothing exceptional. This is vital in understanding why the final phases of Hillary's strategy backfired.

PART 2: THE ACTUAL LOCKER ROOM

Of course, the question is not whether Trump's comments were appropriate for TV. The question is whether they even had a place in locker room conversations, which tend to be more vulgar.

Many actors suggested that they had never heard such talk, even in locker rooms. Actors who came from a drama background may have been telling the truth. The backstage of a play (the "locker room" of a theater) tends to be co-ed. Thus, the nature of the banter tends to be slightly less vulgar than in single sex locker rooms.

But the reality is that many actors have spent plenty of time in single sex locker rooms. They all knew how vulgar locker room comments can be. But they had to maintain their own public images. An actor with a nice-guy public image to maintain would be a fool to admit the true level of locker room vulgarity. It would damage his brand!

In my own life, I have had the opportunity to be in a few locker rooms, ranging from the locker rooms at an all boys private school to those at a very liberal Ivy League college (Brown University). Based on my own experiences and those with whom I have discussed this issue, Trump's comments fall squarely into the category of locker room talk. Specifically, G-rated locker room talk.

Locker room talk often involves a kind of escalating competition of who can say the most disgusting things. Most of it, by the way, does not happen in physical locker rooms, although some of it does.

By the time I was in 8th grade, I had gotten used to people making sexual comments about each other's mothers, various empty brags about unlikely sexual exploits, and all kinds of overtly disgusting and improbable plans. That might not say much for my social milieu, but that is not the strategic question at hand. The question is: how comparatively vulgar were Trump's comments?

At super-liberal Brown University, where I played a semester of Rugby, we had not just locker room talk, but locker room handouts. One handout described various unlikely, offensive, and disgusting "sex positions." I do not remember most of them, but I'm pretty sure I'll never forget the "Donkey Punch." The donkey punch, as its name might suggest, combines anal sex and punching the woman in the head, all in order to increase the pleasure for the man. The other activities on the list were equally outlandish and vulgar. The upperclassmen told us there would be a quiz on the topic.

Of the few things in life I can guarantee: no one on that team, or any other group that saw that somewhat famous list, has ever donkey punched anyone.

"Donkey Punch," because of its outlandish vulgarity, quickly slipped into normal conversation ("I seriously just got donkey punched by that exam.") In fact,

Enron executives used the term "Donkey punch" to refer to price gouging methods! While those executives are by no means pillars of decency, it shows how common such outlandishly offensive terms are, even in business vernacular.

Another popular concept at the time was "the shocker," a hand position of graphic sexual significance. Teams would often pose with all members having their hand in the "shocker" position. Since coaches did not get it, they often let teams get away with it.

By the way, even girls' sports teams would jokingly try to pose with "the shocker" in team photos. In 2006, members of a girls' basketball team in Farmington, Ill., got suspended for having their hands in the "shocker" position during a team photo. Rock star Steven Tyler flashed the hand gesture for a photo that was used in Disney's Hollywood studios for years until people finally noticed the gesture and had it digitally altered in 2016 to an open palm.

Even now, there are many t-shirts that celebrate "the shocker." And, I'm sure, plenty of teams still try to sneak the hand symbol into team photos.

I could continue, but suffice to say that vulgar, aggressive, and even violent sexual humor is common in locker room culture. It may be a better world if this were not the case, but for the purpose of analyzing this election, the commonness of that type of humor is the critical consideration, not whether society needs to be overall changed.

In that context, "grab them by the pussy" would get a 1 out of 10 on the vulgarity scale. Had he used a phrase like "grab the economy by the pussy" during a political speech, that would have been one thing. But poorly timed private ribaldry is just not that unusual.

STRATEGIC MISHANDLING

Media outlets operated under the notion that public speech was still separated from private speech, which it is. But then they went on to apply their overly polite and appropriate rules of public speech to all private speech as well. This heavily backfired. Trump's private speech was well within the bounds of public speech, and so telling the country that such comments were not acceptable in public or private was viewed as idiotic, highly invasive, and controlling.

The tactic was a clear misapplication of the social pressure method. The media wanted to use the comment to destroy Trump's chances, so they attempted to convince everyone that such a statement was unimaginably disturbing. Unfortunately, their audiences had heard much worse.

CLINTON'S CAMPAIGN

When the Clinton campaign began hammering Trump on this issue, they were saying the same thing as the media: "Joking like that in private is no longer acceptable."

Think about what that means. The message to every man and woman is: if you joke around with your buddies in private, and make a joke that's a little off or crass in not quite the right funny way, you can lose major opportunities. That's not something most people are comfortable with.

The Clinton campaign did not realize this any more than the media did, so they kept hammering Trump on this issue. The more they did it, the worse Clinton started looking. Clinton was becoming the thought police, going after a private joke in an era in which crass humor is increasingly popular.

Republicans started withdrawing their endorsements. This just made Republicans look like part of the same thought police. Now Clinton and the Republicans were part of some coalition of prissy hall monitors that were here to ruin you if you make an inappropriate comment. This was not about being politically correct in public, or in the workplace. This was about what you could say in private to your own friends.

People were getting nervous. They were not saying anything, because very few of us would defend in public the jokes we have made in private.

Democrats and Hillary supporters shouted out into the world that this was absolutely the most horrific thing a person could ever possibly say, that it was completely unacceptable, and that it should disqualify a person from pretty much everything in life. In true echo chamber style, the only people who shouted back were those who agreed. "You're right!" they said, "We cannot imagine anyone ever saying anything worse than this in the history of ever. This is just so disturbing."

But the problem is, even they knew they were lying. Everyone of voting age for the 2016 election, including all Democrats, was also alive for the Two Girls One Cup video that went viral in 2007, and plenty of other disgusting, crude, disturbing things. Everyone shouted to the rooftops that Trump's language was so terrible, but no one believed it.

And, it left everyone pretty scared. In a world of dead baby jokes and sexual bragging, millions of people were afraid for their lifestyles if the Democrats gained control and banned them from thinking anything that was not PG.

PRIVACY RIGHTS

There is one more important bit of context we need to add. Privacy rights were becoming increasingly more important in the years and months leading up to the 2016 election. Despite Democrats and Republicans (including Trump) denouncing him, Edward Snowden remained extremely popular. People were already on edge because of NSA mass surveillance, the Patriot Act, etc.

Now combine that kind of mass surveillance with this new rule that if you say something vulgar in private, it can damage your business and political opportunities. And keep in mind that many of these fears are growing and mixing in the individual unconscious minds.

When the tapes first came out, Trump looked like a greasy and disgusting man. But when the Clinton campaign and the RNC started hammering him, he now became someone being attacked for a private joke.

Among those watching, there were a lot more who had made crass jokes than who had not. The more Trump was attacked, the more they sided with him.

But they said nothing. After all, actors, celebrities, and social pressure said that those types of jokes were not even okay in private. Each individual voter was afraid to stand up against the entire media, the Democratic and Republican parties, and countless other major social figures.

But when Trump did, he basically became their defender. The entire media and political establishment attacked him. He attacked right back. Furiously, unabashedly, relentlessly. The media and political establishment kept attacking. He kept fighting back. Each time, he was the hero of the 99.9% of people who said crass things in private at some point in their lives, but were too shy to defend those things in public.

Admittedly, the Clinton campaign was in a difficult position. Had they just let it slide, they would have been seen as condoning the comments. But their tactic made them look like thought police, and made Trump look like the defender of the right to joke around with your friends. The Clinton campaign ended up looking humorless and prissy.

In hindsight, one option would have been to shift over to a deeper flaw while casting themselves as the defenders of freedom. For example, Hillary could have said something like, "I do not personally find Mr. Trump's comments humorous, but I will defend his right to say what he wants in private. I will not, however, tolerate his claim that he can require all Muslims to register like Jews in pre-war Germany, or allow him to separate families through irresponsible, anti-immigration measures." A tactic like that would have made Hillary look strong and tolerant, and made Trump look like an immature degenerate.

A SIMILAR STORY

In the 1990s, cigarette companies lost a lawsuit. As part of the lawsuit, they had to fund an anti-cigarette televi-sion campaign. They were only too happy to oblige. After all, cigarette advertising on TV was not allowed before.

Furthermore, they knew that if the government advertised against anything, they would make that thing more popular. Of course, they were right. The anti-cigarette ads caused cigarette sales among teenagers to spike. When obviously out of touch people design ads that say, "you better not smoke, kid," it is just going to encourage smoking. As WebMD put it: "What's the best way to convince a teenager that smoking is a great idea? Tell him his parents want him to stop."

The same was true with the Trump tapes. An old campaign clearly out of touch with social reality kept insisting that private dirty jokes between friends disqualified a person from politics and business. That was essentially advertising for Trump.

TWO TYPES OF COOL

There are two general categories of cool men: Golden Boys and Bad Boys. You'll find both types portrayed on TV, and both kinds are popular.

Golden Boys are the nice guys, but not the kind that finish last. They are charming, socially aware, and comforting. Jim from *The Office*, Shawn from *Psych*, and Ted from *Better of Ted* are examples.

Bad Boys are deliberately crude, borderline bullies, and often drunk. Sterling Archer from *Archer*, all the characters in *It is Always Sunny in Philadelphia*, and all the characters from *The League* are examples.

Bad Boys and Golden Boys are both popular. The same viewers often watch shows featuring each type.

Golden Boys are often more charming while Bad Boys are more charismatic. Bad Boys tend to spend most of any show shamelessly pursuing sex and money. Given the huge ratings of these shows, it is safe to say that many people find that relatable. Golden Boys spend most of a show pursuing a love interest or trying to look out for the underdog. Given the huge popularity of those shows, it is safe to say many people find that relatable as well.

Obama is a Golden Boy. That's his entire brand. He does positive things for positive reasons. Even though he admitted to using marijuana and possibly cocaine, one imagines that he found a wholesome, positive way to do it.

Trump is a Bad Boy. He always has been. He's shameless in his pursuit of money, sex, and power. When he talks about trying to seduce married women, but not getting there, it is not a big deal. That's what we expect. Long before he ran for president, he was a recurring guest on Howard Stern's talk show, which tended to focus exclusively on crude topics.

Trump's reality show signature line is "You're Fired." Few businessmen seem to relish that part as much as he does, or make it so entertaining.

He's been married multiple times, and his current wife is only 11 years older than his daughter. He married her, we can assume, largely because of her physical attractiveness.

The crude things we heard on tape simply did not involve any change in who we saw Trump as. Sure, he was crude, but he was consistent. People respect consistency.

If we'd heard Obama say something like that, it would have destroyed his brand entirely. Obama talking about attempting aggressive seduction on married women, or boasting about grabbing their genitals, even in private, would have made his entire image a lie. But with Trump, it just confirmed that he was a Bad Boy, that he was just as crude in private as in public.

SEXUAL ASSAULT ALLEGATIONS

Words are one thing; actions are another. Plenty of men make crude jokes. Far fewer actually do or attempt sexual assault.

After the tapes came out, one sexual assault allegation after another came out against Trump. Logically, it should have been the end of his campaign. So why wasn't it?

Of the hundreds of people I have talked to about this, the group that seems the most completely flab-bergasted by this is millennial women. Some, infuriated, believe that sexual assault is clearly now totally acceptable in the eyes of the majority of Americans. They have become convinced that Rape Culture is alive and well, that our country has now completely normalized and accepted many types of rape, including date rape, marital rape, and rape obtained without consent because the woman was drunk.

A popular saying: rape is not always a stranger in a dark alley with a gun. It can be a friend, a date, an authority figure, a lover, or even a husband. Any individual act of sex requires consent, and without active consent, the act of sex is rape.

On a strict, technical level, most people agree actually agree with this, despite what Trump's win might suggest. No one should ever be forced. Morally, most people agree.

But outrage levels tend to vary based on the nature of the situation. In general, the word rape generates outrage, disgust, and hate. But the specific type of rape that generates that is the hypothetical stranger in a dark alley rape. That is a case of an innocent, careful woman being violated. It is the horrific acts done in rape-torture rooms in Iraq. That is the rape that immediately generates raw, unfiltered fury.

The other kinds of rape do not generate the same emotional response. I'm not saying that they should not; I'm saying that they do not.

Imagine this: suppose I carefully lock the door of my house, and have a safe in which I keep my grandfather's pocket watch. Then, one day, burglars break in, use some new technology to open the safe, and steal the watch. You might feel bad for me.

On the other hand, suppose I take that same pocket watch, and put it on the very edge of my property, one millimeter from the busy sidewalk. It gets stolen.

In a moral sense, the crime is exactly the same. It was my possession, and I kept it on my property. But you might just not feel that bad for me. You will agree that in a perfect world it would not have happened, and that it should not have happened. The police will take a report, but they are not going to take it very seriously. Yes, I got robbed. But I was not really trying to not get robbed.

Ideally, I shouldn't have to try to not get robbed. I just should not be robbed. If I want to fan myself with $100 bills and walk through a rough part of a city, I should be able to. But doing so would be considered reckless. In acting like that, I simply cannot expect the same sympathy and outrage as the person who got his safe burglarized.

At a basic, emotional level, most people feel the same way about rape. I'm not saying that they should, but they do. Even those who are deeply a part of safe space culture know that stranger rape generates more sympathy than marital rape. People are more outraged when a jogger is raped by a stranger than when a wife is raped by her husband. In fact, before 1984 in New York, there was a marital exemption to rape law.

For decades now, many groups have been focusing so heavily on non-stranger rape that it has become equal in their eyes to stranger rape. They expect and demand the same level of outrage. Most people go along with it, since no one really wants to defend an abusive husband.

If a woman is in a man's room, physically enticing him, he does not have the right to force himself on her. But a woman doing that will get less sympathy than a young mom picking up groceries who gets raped by a stranger.

Many of the rapes happening on college campuses are based on various technicalities. For example, if a woman is drunk, her consent does not count. Even if she is enthusiastic or aggressive about sex while drunk, a man who has sex with her in that state would be guilty of rape. To use the gold pocket watch metaphor, it would be like if I got drunk, insistently gave the watch to a stranger, and then said I'd been robbed. Technically, the stranger should have been decent and refused a gift from a drunk. But I'm not going to get much sympathy for that.

There has been a major psychological backlash against the expectation that every single type of acquaintance rape get the same outrage as stranger rape does. On social media, posts about Rape Culture generate hundreds of comments about how women need to take some responsibility, and not drunkenly put themselves into dangerous situations. In my experience, most of these posts actually come from women. Part of this is because older women expect younger women to learn the same level of responsibility that they had to learn. Part of it is because men are way too scared to say anything.

Various men's rights groups aggressively speak out against the seemingly one-sided rape laws. The groups get aggressively slammed for doing so. Most famously, a satirical post from activist Roosh V was taken literally, and subjected to all manner of reprisal. In the wake of the media firestorm, I looked up the original article. In it, he satirically suggested that if rape were legal on private property, it would give women an incentive to be responsible about where they went and with whom. It was written in the tone of Swift's *A Modest Proposal*. It is easy to find online, and blatantly obviously a satire.

What's interesting is that it was not just "crazy radical feminist groups" who had this interpretation, and worked to shut down his meetups. The *Washington Times*, the *Daily Mail*, *ABC*, *The Los Angeles Times, The BBC*, and others reported on it, and various mayors and immigration officials worked to block his meetups. In the UK, legislation was proposed to ban his meetings as hate crimes.

Obviously, the media attention drove record numbers to his website, but the point is: there were huge numbers for whom his message resonated.

Politically, all of this helps explain why the various allegations of sexual assault did literally no damage to Trump at all. Universities and Anti Rape-Culture groups have pushed the pendulum past where most people agree. Their view, that victims acting recklessly have no contributory negligence, is just not where people are right now. There may come a time when society is such that a woman can walk nude and drunk through a frat party, and go completely unmolested. I hope that day comes soon. It will be a testament to human decency.

But those who expect the world to be like that when it is not have made people increasingly skeptical of reports of rape.

With Trump, Democrats presented information in a way designed to appeal to very liberal Democrats. They called him a rapist, because his ex wife, Ivana, had filed suit against him for rape while they were married (which she later retracted, saying that she had not meant rape in the literal sense, but rather in an emotional sense). The media listed one event after another.

But there was a pattern that beleaguered and suspicious people noticed. First, they supposedly happened decades ago, but only came out during campaign season. Second, most happened in public places, around friends and acquaintances. One woman asserted that Trump had tried to unsuccessfully assault her repeatedly over a period of weeks, leaving many people wondering why she didn't just leave after the first time. Another happened in the first class cabin of a plane, leaving voters wondering why the victim did not push the flight attendant call button.

The list was long, but it was not the kind of assault people take seriously in private.

Of course, in public, they were quick to decry all of these possible allegations. But in the privacy of the voting booth, I doubt it had any effect.

As an important note: people who are assaulted are often so confused and taken aback by the whole thing that they often freeze up. The psychological impact is traumatizing, and people often do not know what to do. They do not want to be publicly humiliated. They may be in denial about what happened. A personal violation, even when it happens on a romantic date, is so personally wrenching that the immediate responses of the victim are highly unpredictable. Sometimes it legitimately takes weeks or months for a person to admit even to themselves that they have been raped.

Unfortunately, those psychological nuances were not on the radar of most voters.

It is worth mentioning, however, that it would be beneficial to move society in a direction in which acquaintance rape never happens. It would be ideal to be in a society in which women simply do not have to worry about being sexually assaulted.

Right now, it sounds far fetched to most Americans. But the fact is that many behaviors we take for granted in America seem far fetched to people all over the world. For example, many people use their cell phones at night in America. But in many parts of Brazil, holding an iPhone in public is inviting robbery. In America, we can wear fancy watches and jewelry. People can wear wedding rings in public, or even engagement rings!

We have come to an incredible level of safety in many parts of the country. Certainly, there are some cities in which you have to be very careful. But in most parts of the country, talking on the phone is not a guarantee of robbery.

How amazing would it be if we could do the same with rape? How great would it be if a woman could go to a man's house at any hour of the day and have no more reason to fear rape than to fear being eaten by a cannibal?

We are not there yet. Right now, some people are still taking ill advised risks. But if we keep working, I believe we'll get there. On the way, though, it is important to live in the real world, to recognize the current social landscape, especially when crafting political arguments and attack campaigns.

EMAILS

When viewing Trump's scandal, Hillary's email scandal seemed, to many Democrats, extremely minor. Of all the election scandals in history, Hillary's email scandal was also the single hardest to understand. Throughout the entire campaign, no one knew why you would or would not use a private server for classified emails. They did not know if she was being accused of carelessness or espionage. They did not know what was in the emails – nuclear codes or frustration at her daughter.

At least Bill Clinton's scandals had been comprehensible. And yet, Bill Clinton's scandals did not seem to hurt him as much as Hillary's seemed to hurt her. Neither did Trump's. Despite the incomprehensible content, her scandal was apparently more damaging. How is that possible?

I once heard an interview with Richard Dawkins, author of *The God Delusion*. The interviewer asked him how many people he felt he had persuaded to give up their belief in god. Dawkins said that he thought he had actually convinced very few people, but rather had given people psychological permission to not believe in god. Those people had never really believed in the first place, but had just gone along with it because of either social pressure or inner psychological compulsion. Now an important authority figure said it was totally okay to not believe in god. They were happy to jump at the chance to embrace their true beliefs.

The political psychology of the emails was very similar.

People did not like Hillary. They saw her as arrogant, smug, and phony. Unfortunately, even in the privacy of an election booth, smugness and phoniness are not always sufficient reasons to vote against someone, especially if her opponent has been accused of sexual assault, been a general boor and bigot for the entire election, etc. Voters needed an excuse to do what they so fundamentally wanted to do. Literally any excuse would do. The email scandal got the job done.

I'm sure there were at least a dozen cybersecurity nerds who understood what the big hoopla was about. Maybe half of them actually based their voting decision on that knowledge.

But for everyone else, the emails were an excuse to vote against a person whom they just simply did not like.

The Clinton Foundation scandal worked in pretty much the same way. No one really understood what, if anything, the scandal was. But there was at least a reasonable likelihood of...something probably unpleasant. Even if that likelihood was tiny, it gave people psychological permission to vote against a candidate they disliked.

Hillary's campaign attempted to address the allegations. But they did not appear to understand what they were actually up against. They thought that if they established the preponderance of evidence in Hillary's favor, or discredited the opposition, that would be enough.

Various politicians spoke out in Hillary's defense. Even William Weld, the Libertarian candidate for Vice President and former governor of Massachusetts, went on CNN defending her and calling more recent rounds of investigations inappropriate (in doing so, of course, he antagonized many in the Libertarian Party).

But it was not enough. Voters were not weighing the evidence. They were not "voting as jurors." They were just looking for any excuse that would give them psychological permission to vote against Hillary.

VOTING AND POLLING

SANDERS AND THE NEW STRATEGIC VOTERS

One reason that corporations, unions, and other special interests have so much influence on politics: they have long memories, and think long term. Voters usually think one election at a time. Special Interest groups have multi-election strategies.

Politicians often break promises to voters. They rarely break promises to corporations. Corporations remember. Voters forget.

Over the last years, this has been changing. Voters have started looking at politics over multiple elections. They have realized that they can withhold votes in order to pressure political establishments.

This has a major effect on a popular bait and switch technique used in politics. Here's how the usual strategy works. A political party allows, or even encourages, a populist, anti-establishment candidate to gain traction. In 2012, the Republican Party did this with Ron Paul. In 2016, the Democratic party did this with Bernie Sanders.

The populist candidate brings millions of new people, particularly young voters, to the party.

Then the populist candidate loses (often with help from the political machine). The RNC did all kinds of things to block Ron Paul delegates at the 2012 convention, and the DNC may have had a similar role in helping Bernie Sanders lose in 2016.

Once the populist candidate loses in the primary, the party leadership tries to get those supporters to vote for the establishment candidate. Those voters had to register with the party to vote in the primary. They have already psychologically committed to the party. It should be pretty easy to get them to switch from the anti-establishment candidate to the establishment candidate.

But during the last two election cycles, it has not been working that well. Even when the anti-establishment candidate endorses the establishment candidate, the bait and switch is falling short. Ron Paul refused to endorse Mitt Romney in 2012. Bernie Sanders, however, did endorse Hillary Clinton in 2016. But both Romney and Clinton lost.

The first reason this did not work is obvious. When the DNC and RNC tried to make the establishment candidate win using underhanded methods, that obviously offended the supporters of the populist candidate. That's not rocket science. But even when Sanders endorsed

Clinton, that was not enough. Even when he asked his
supporters to vote for Clinton, it was not enough.

The second reason is policy. The difference between
Sanders and Clinton in policy were actually quite significant. While a side by side comparison suggests that they
have nearly identical views, they actually differ hugely in
one area: war. Sanders does not believe in using the military
as a world police. Clinton does. That critical policy difference brought many independent voters to the Sanders
campaign. It also caused many Democratic voters to refuse
to vote for Hillary in the general election.

For both moral and financial reasons, war is losing
popularity. While a bait and switch tactic can work in politics, it cannot work when candidates differ on such a major
issue. Many antiwar Sanders supporters simply could not be
convinced to vote for Clinton.

To understand this further, it is important to
consider how the populist campaigns started in the first
place. Those campaigns usually attract relatively high-
information voters. The populist voters usually do enough
research to find out about the existence of the populist
candidate in the first place. These are the kinds of voter-
nerds who actually vote in the primary elections.

Many voters first learn about these populist candidates on social media. That means that they will later have
access to other relevant information through social media.

Those who vote for the anti-establishment candidates think deeply about political strategy. They do not just go to the polls and vote blindly for every Democrat or every Republican. Those who end up supporting the establishment candidate do so after thinking about it carefully.

Supporters of anti-establishment candidates usually know of the existence of third party candidates. Many end up supporting them.

Others simply refuse to vote. They are working to pressure their own parties in the long term. For example, in 2016, many Sanders supporters simply did not vote. They were telling the DNC, "If you want us to vote for a Democrat, give us a Democrat worth voting for."

Voters are becoming more savvy and less gullible. More and more are realizing that if they want to influence politics the way corporations do, they will have to think long-term the way corporations do. They are not willing to get caught up in the, "We have to vote for Hillary to stop Trump" dramatics.

Instead, they are thinking about policy. Those who want to see an end to the War on Drugs will only vote for candidates who will move policy in that direction. Those who want to see an end to military involvement in foreign civil wars will only vote for candidates who will move policy in that direction. On social media, "Your Vote is Your Voice" has become a popular saying. People are often exercising that voice by supporting candidates with the views they support, even when that candidate has a lower probability of winning.

This has obviously been great for third parties. This year, both the Libertarian and Green parties had unusually high vote totals. In fact, the Libertarian Party had the highest third party vote totals in 20 years, since Ross Perot.

Strategically, the DNC and RNC should stop treating high information voters like low information voters. There are plenty of voters who will blindly vote Democratic or Republican. There are also plenty of voters who can be scared into Voting X to Stop Y.

But there are also plenty of voters who are voting strategically to pressure their party into supporting the policies that the voters want. The DNC and RNC should be very careful about alienating them, or becoming overconfident under the assumption that these voters will vote on party lines no matter what.

In fact, this principle now even applies to third parties! Many Libertarians took issue with some of Vice Presidential candidate William Weld's statements and refused to vote for him! Even in alternative parties, the establishment ignores its base at its own risk.

Polling during the 2016 election cycle was so off that newspapers and polling have been reconsidering all aspects of their polling methodology. On November 13, 2016 *The New York Times* issued a letter from the executive editor and publisher that promised to rededicate the *Times* to an accurate and unbiased method of news reporting.

In one part of the letter that made international news, they promise:

"As we reflect on the momentous result, and the months of reporting and polling that preceded it, we aim to rededicate ourselves to the fundamental mission of *Times* journalism. That is to report America and the world honestly, without fear or favor, striving always to understand and reflect all political perspectives and life experiences in the stories that we bring to you."

But the fact is their polling method, in its core, is simply not sufficient to account for the volatility of modern politics, fueled by a 24 hour news cycle and worldwide social media. Their current tools are not up to the task. As a political strategist with an actuarial background, I have some insights on how to make polls that more accurately reflect voter behavior.

Current polling methods basically take snapshots of the current situation. They let you know, basically, who currently favors whom. This is the most rudimentary level

of statistical measurement, one that is rarely used when
any amount of money is at stake. When money is at stake,
as it is with large insurance companies, more sophisticated
mathematical models are used.

For example, when you buy car insurance, you
answer all kinds of questions, including what your job is,
how far you travel for work, what kind of car you have, etc.
Those are used to predict the probability that you will be in
an accident, and how costly such an accident is likely to be.

If car insurance companies used the kind of "statistics" used by the *New York Times*, they would basically just
ask, "Are you currently having a car accident?" It would be
an insane way to predict future outcomes.

For mathematical predictions to work, snapshot
statistics must give way to behaviorally predictive statistics. There are many people with decades of experience in
predictive statistics, which is used throughout the entire
financial sector. Political polling companies can learn from
those methods to create more reliable models.

Those models must consider many variables more
carefully. First, it is important to measure the impact of
third parties. For 2016, state by state, the number of Gary
Johnson votes was almost always greater than the difference
between Trump and Hillary votes. Thus, this information is
highly relevant in determining the outcome.

Current polls, even ones that include third party candidates, are not measuring their impact accurately. Their simplistic approach does not take into account the probability of second choice voting. A poll that includes all candidates will almost certainly measure the respondent's first choice. If you also ask a third party voter who they prefer between the Democratic and Republican candidate, you will get that person's second or third choice. However, you will not get any sense of how likely they are to defect from their first choice to their second choice.

For example, suppose that 90% of Gary Johnson voters who had Hillary as a second choice switched, but only 1% of Gary Johnson voters who had Trump as a second choice switched, that information is obviously relevant.

Additionally, third party candidates tend to poll much higher earlier in an election cycle. They may poll 20% early in the cycle, but only get 2% on election day. Where that remaining 18% goes is highly significant to the outcome of any election.

Measuring this probability poses a unique challenge. If you just ask how likely a person is to vote for their second choice, most people will say 0%. People like to be seen as strong and principled, with an unbreakable word. However, there are ways to get this information.

Some polling experts have suggested simply asking who the respondent voted for in the previous election.

Those who voted for a third party candidate may be more likely to vote for a third party candidate in the current election. This method would probably improve accuracy, but it would not entirely fix the problem, given the huge fluctuations in third party vote totals that we have seen in recent elections. For example, in 2012, 1 million people voted for Gary Johnson. In 2016, 4 million people voted for him.

Another way to judge is to ask what issues matter the most. If ending the War on Drugs was the most important issue for a Johnson voter, the odds of defecting in 2016 would be almost zero, given that neither Hillary nor Trump had that as a policy. If the most important issue for a Johnson voter was ending Obamacare, he may have defected to Trump. If his most important issue was candidate integrity, and he perceived Hillary and Trump to be equally untrustworthy, then he probably would not have switched. If a Jill Stein supporter's most important issue was increasing the minimum wage, he may have switched to Hillary. None of these are guarantees, but with enough data, percentage conversion rates can be more reliably predicted.

It is also important to collect data on character voters, issue voters, and probabilistic voters. Character voters vote primarily based on personality; they want a decent, trustworthy person. They generally care less about particular issues. Issue voters care more about issues than about character or personality. Probabilistic voters are highly influenced by a candidate's chance of winning (they are more likely to vote for candidates with a higher probability of winning). Understanding which category a voter is most likely to fall into can help create more reliable polling. A probabilistic voter will be influenced by vastly different concerns than an issue voter.

Additionally, the surroundings of a voter must be taken into account. Pollsters need to determine what setting the respondent is in, who can hear or observe the questioning. For example, three hours after the "Grab them by the pussy" tape leaked, a father who still planned to vote for Trump might not say so in front of his daughter. Incorporating relevant correction or reliability factors will help make polling more accurate.

Current polling methods are clearly obsolete. Polling firms should invest in creating more nuanced behavioral models (similar to the predictive models used by insurance companies). Insurance companies can lose millions or billions of dollars if their predictive models are not accurate. Thus, they collect enough data on enough variables to predict accurately. If polling companies start using actuarial style predictive models which attempt to predict likely future behavior, rather than just taking snapshot polls of current moods, they will be more reliable and more useful to all candidates and voters. Given modern data collection and computational abilities, there is no reason for polls to be so inaccurate.

But to accomplish this, polling organizations must drop political bias from polling. They must work to make their questions as unbiased as possible, and ask policy questions that cover all major viewpoints.

There are always political reasons to slant polls. But doing so muddies the data and reduces reliability. Complete, objective polling that takes all relevant factors into account is the only way to have a possibility of accurate prediction.

WHY IS THERE POLLING BIAS AT ALL?

People routinely try to slant survey questions to get the answers they want. Sometimes they are even more blatant. As a member of the leadership of the Libertarian Party, I'm often part of the struggle to get third party candidates included in the polls. Obviously, they are not excluded for scientific reasons. Including all choices will clearly make polls more accurate. Third parties are excluded for political reasons.

The questions themselves are designed for political reasons as well. Some pollsters lean conservative, and try to make the Republicans seem more ahead. Others do the same with Democrats.

It is all part of the accepted battleground of politics.

But the problem is, when you develop decades of experience slanting polls, you fail to develop the skills needed to make polls accurate. As culture changes, pollsters need to adapt. Today, more people use cellphones instead of landlines. This often makes landline-only polling ridiculously inaccurate. Some people (like me) rarely answer cell phone or landline calls, making them only available via text message. These types of changes require constant innovation in the field of polling accuracy.

But polling companies have not been working on that skill. They have been working on the skill of political slant. They have gotten really good at it. In fact, they got so good at fooling voters with those polls that they accidentally fooled themselves.

But voters are becoming harder to fool. The more blatantly idiotic polling is forced on them, the more they distrust polls in general. Especially after such a shocking, literally a completely unpredicted, win by Trump, voters will be far more suspicious of polls in elections to come. So even if the political landscape demands highly subjective polling to help a particular politician stay in power, the people in this country will start to more aggressively demand real, factual polling to help them stay abreast of the truth.

THE ROLE OF THIRD PARTIES

Democrats and Republicans publicly say that third parties are irrelevant to politics. But their actions tell a different story. They go out of their way to try to remove third party candidates from debates and from the ballot, spending millions of their own dollars to do so. Third parties spend hundreds of thousands of dollars in individual states to collect the monumental numbers of signatures needed to stay on the ballot, and Democrats and Republicans often take third parties to court to challenge the validity of the signatures.

In some races, the concern is that a third party candidate might win. But in the presidential race, the larger concern is that a third party candidate may be more attractive to voters who would have otherwise voted for a Democratic or Republican candidate. This can cause the Democrats or Republicans to lose votes. Even though those votes do not go to their direct opponent, if they lose enough votes, they still lose the election.

Third parties generally exist because they either offer some popular policies or combinations of policies that the Republican and Democratic parties do not offer.

Ending the War on Drugs has long been a policy, spearheaded by Libertarians, that has attracted voters to the Libertarian party. Freedom of Marriage was also spearheaded by Libertarians and eventually became so popular that Democrats adopted it as well. The Libertarian party also offers voters the combination of gay rights and second amendment rights, a combination not found in either of the two major parties right now. Similarly, the Green Party advocates a combination of opposition to war, taxpayer funded college tuition, and strict environmentalism not found in other parties.

Third Party voters tend to be high information voters. In other words, they study a bit more than the average voter. That's basically a prerequisite to knowing that third parties exist in the first place. You do not hear about third parties as much on TV or in traditional media, so you need to do more research to learn about them.

Historically, third party candidates tend to poll much higher early in the election cycle than later. There are a few major reasons for this. One, third parties are generally not included in debates. The presidential debates are a critical part of election marketing. Candidates are finally side by side, live. Undecided voters often make decisions by watching the debates, and other voters often switch sides.

Another reason: as elections approach, voters get increasingly worried that the Republican or Democratic candidate they like less will win. For example, they might end up voting for Clinton to beat Trump, or voting for Trump to beat Clinton.

Some third party voters have one policy that matters to them more than any other. The end up voting for whichever major party candidate supports that policy.

Thus, while a third party candidate may poll at 20 percent early in the election cycle, he may end up getting only 2 percent of the vote. Both the Democrats and Republicans scramble to get as many of those "defector" votes as possible.

Early in the election, Trump laid the groundwork to capture some of those third party defector votes. Hillary did not.

A few days before the election, Bryan Cranston, star of *Breaking Bad*, released a video opposing Trump. One thing he pointed out was that was that Trump was not at all specific about his policies. He said that Trump only vaguely indicated that he would make things great, and it would be huuuge (with extra u's). But Trump knew that there are two types of voters: high information voters and low information voters. High information voters want policy details. Low information voters want charisma. On TV he presented his aggressive, authentic, unafraid, charismatic side.

But on his website, he was pretty clear about policy, and how it would work. He was clear about repealing Obamacare, ending gun free zones, and eliminating the Department of Education. He even explained exactly how he would get Mexico to pay for a wall on our southern border. Despite his reputation, it was actually surprisingly detailed.

He'd been studying elections, including third party politics, for years. In fact, in the past he even considered running for president as the Reform Party candidate (the Reform Party was started by Ross Perot.)

So his website was covered with lures to attract third party defectors. He knew that if he could get some of the millions who would defect, it could tip the balance.

He knew that many voters wanted to see an end to the Department of Education, particularly given the unpopularity of Common Core. He also knew that many voters wanted to see an end to Obamacare. So he made sure to set lures for those voters.

In fact, he even went further, discussing changing or even eliminating the U.S. participation in NATO, a very hard line position that would appeal to even diehard libertarians.

Hillary did not really do that. Instead, she tried to capture the Sanders supporters. Unfortunately, she did not really try to appeal to them through either policy or through personal presentation. Sanders talked about ending the War on Drugs and ending foreign wars. Hillary opposed both of these policies. Nor did she try to present herself as trustworthy and authentic the way Sanders had. And she certainly did not have any of Sanders' anti-establishment credibility. She basically argued that Sanders

was a Democrat, and she was a Democrat, so Sanders voters
should vote for her. This is not a great way to go after high
information voters.

Gary Johnson, the Libertarian Party candidate,
understood the idea that Sanders voters were moved
by trustworthiness, nice-guy appearance, and anti-
establishment views. Hundreds of thousands of Sanders
supporters that the Hillary campaign had banked on went
to Johnson. Another several hundred thousand went to Jill
Stein, the Green Party candidate.

Early polling showed that over 20 percent of
Sanders supporters planned to vote for Johnson. While
Sanders himself campaigned to lower this number, he
could not bring it down enough.

Many observers could not understand what was
happening. Gary Johnson's policies, while they had some
overlap, were often diametrically opposed to those of Sanders.
Sure, they both wanted to reduce or end the War on Drugs.
But one of Sanders' main policy selling points was that he
wanted to have government pay for college. Johnson wanted to
eliminate the existing government funding for college.

But that did not matter as much. Johnson also
understood authenticity. He came across as trustworthy,
nice, and honest. Trump also seemed authentic, but was too
aggressive and arrogant to get many Sanders' supporters.

In the end, the majority of Sanders supporters voted for Hillary. But quite a few also voted for Johnson and Stein. Had Hillary presented as authentic instead of phony, she would probably have gotten more.

In this landmark election, third parties played a much larger role than the two major parties might have hoped.

UNEMPLOYMENT MYTHS

Bias, of course, is not limited to polling. One particularly important instance of statistical bias in this election centered around unemployment.

This election's Democratic and Republican narratives both focused on unemployment. Republicans argued that jobs were being lost to outsourcing and immigration. Democrats focused on low employment numbers among young people and minorities.

Somehow Trump's message resonated, while the Democratic message did not. To many political strategists and to voters, this seems bizarre.

Hillary's campaign stated that, "roughly one in ten Americans between the ages of 16 and 24 is unemployed, more than twice the national average. And these numbers hide devastating racial disparities: the unemployment rate for African American millennials between the ages of 16-24 is roughly twice that of white millennials while the unemployment rate for Latino millennials is more than 10 percent higher."

On the other hand, Trump's said, "Look at how much African American communities are suffering from Democratic control. ... Fifty-eight percent of your youth is unemployed, what the hell do you have to lose?"

Why did one message work and the other fail?

THE UNRELIABILITY OF UNEMPLOYMENT DATA

The Department of Labor has long been derided for under-reporting unemployment numbers. They look at the number of people seeking jobs, divided by the total number of people who are either seeking jobs or employed. Who is not included? People who may want a job, but have given up on their active search for one. In economics, they are referred to as "Discouraged Workers."

It is not easy to accurately count that number. Some people were looking for jobs and then stopped, not because they gave up, but because they got married. Or because they started a black market business. Or they started a respectable business, but are being paid under the table, in cash. So while the Department of Labor is almost by definition underreporting unemployment, it is not easy to say by how much.

And of course, this method of calculation makes unemployment look lower, which is very good for the president in office. Every president want to be known as the president who brought down unemployment.

Thus, at a basic level, the Trump campaign tended to overstate unemployment, to make Obama's policies look bad. After all, it was assumed that Clinton's policies would be similar to Obama's.

Similarly, the Clinton campaign generally understated unemployment, in order to make Obama's policies look good. Specifically, she used the inherently deflated figures presented by the department of labor.

Thus, while both Trump and Clinton addressed unemployment, Clinton generally did so more moderately.

THE UNEMPLOYMENT PARADOX

Despite high unemployment among many groups, there are actually plenty of jobs that employers are struggling to fill.

The problem is that now many people, particularly young people, feel entitled to their preferred lifestyle. Earlier this year, the *New York Times* reported that many employers in Savannah, GA, including lumberyards and other labor intensive businesses, are having difficulty finding people who are able pass a drug test. It has become such an issue that, "In August, Gov. Nathan Deal of

Georgia promised to develop a program to help because so many business owners tell him 'the No. 1 reason they can't hire enough workers is they can't find enough people to pass a drug test.'"

Can you imagine people in any other era refusing to give up drugs, even if that meant not getting a job? The biggest issue is marijuana, which is not even physically addictive. It is purely a lifestyle choice. Given the choice between a job and marijuana, people are literally choosing marijuana. The article further explains that in states like Colorado, even before marijuana was legalized, "to find a roofer or a painter that can pass a drug test is unheard-of", according to the owner of a Colorado painting and roofing company. He added, "As soon as I say 'criminal background check,' or 'drug test,' they're out the door."

As a small business owner myself, I have seen how difficult it can be to find people to even show up for a scheduled job interview. In other words, while there certainly are people who are unemployed, the shortage of jobs is not the only cause, and is possibly not even the primary cause.

Trump, who had extensive private sector experience, understood that there were many different types of unemployment. He understood that going after middle aged men whose manufacturing jobs had been outsourced would be much more effective than going after younger people who simply preferred marijuana to entry level employment.

NON-UNIFORMITY OF UNEMPLOYMENT

There is a second dimension to unemployment that Trump got, but Hillary did not. Unemployment is not the same in every county. Some areas have unemployment close to zero. Others have unemployment near 30 percent.

Trump tended to massively overstate unemployment in his national speeches. Hillary tended to understate it in her national speeches. It made sense: Hillary wanted to argue that Obama's policies were working, and Trump wanted to argue that they were not working.

This ended up working out well for Trump.

Economists describe the difference between a depression and a recession as follows: When your neighbor loses his job, the country is in a recession. When you lose your job, the country is in a depression. People always care a lot more about their own situation, and extrapolate a lot more from it.

The same is true of unemployment. If you're unemployed, as far as you're concerned, the unemployment rate is 100%. If you have a job you like, it might as well be 0%.

Unemployment is only a major political issue for the unemployed. Trump's aggressive statements on

unemployment validated the experiences of the unemployed
and their families, and promised to fix them. Hillary's
claim that unemployment was at an all time low basically
denied their experience. Sure, when she was talking locally
in areas with high unemployment, she probably mentioned
it. But it was the national speeches that everyone saw.

Those who were employed just did not really care if
Trump overstated the numbers. Numerical accuracy was not
an issue for them. He did not lose any votes by overstating
it, and he gained plenty.

Even math nerds did not care. Given the challenge
of calculating the actual number of discouraged workers,
unemployment numbers mostly become a kind of interesting puzzle. Since every single reported number, whether
Trump's or the Department of Labor's, is completely wrong,
overstating the numbers does not really affect credibility. If
anything, the fact that Trump pointed out the technically
correct fact that the Department of Labor underreports
true unemployment may have increased his credibility.

COULD SANDERS HAVE WON?

As people examine why Hillary lost, many are now arguing
that Sanders could have won had he been given the chance.

Sanders had the anti-establishment presentation.
He was aggressive, and did not seem phony.

His policies would probably have hurt him. While they were very popular with the youngest voters, they were much less so with everyone else. Most people would not want the expense of paying for everyone else's college tuitions, especially after they had finished paying off their own college loans.

He was a lot more likable than Hillary, and presented a much clearer vision. However, that vision would have scared most voters. It may have done well in the Democratic primaries, but the large number of independents in the general election would not have responded as well.

My guess is that he probably would not have done much better than Hillary, and quite possibly a lot worse. America was already barely tolerating one socialist leaning policy (Obamacare). Advocating many more probably would not have gone over well.

His likability and anti-establishment credentials would probably have helped. But I do not think Americans would have accepted his policy vision. While charismatic, Sanders is not as charismatic as Obama. It would have taken at least that level of charisma to get people to vote for the policies Sanders supported.

THE REPUBLICAN LEADERSHIP

Why didn't Republican voters follow the Republican leadership? When the Republican congressional, senatorial, and gubernatorial establishment bailed on Trump, why didn't voters also bail?

As it turns out, Republican voters did follow the Republican leadership. The press just does not know where the Republican leadership actually is.

Most conservative voters have probably seen one or two clips of Paul Ryan. They might remember Governor Kasich as "that one guy in the debates who was not very good at debating." They may have seen a YouTube video of Mitch McConnell. They may have seen a quote somewhere from Reince Priebus.

But those are not the real leaders of the Republican Party or the conservative movement. If you want to find them, you need to listen to talk radio. Influencers like Rush Limbaugh and Mark Levin preach to millions of listeners every weekday for 3 hour segments.

Many conservative voters listen to them daily. As a podcaster myself, let me tell you: these guys are the best of the best. Their shows are persuasive and insightful, and build coherent arguments and narratives. They are masters of spin and persuasion. And they made their message clear: Vote Trump to beat Hillary.

Evan McMullin, who initially polled at 20 percent a few weeks before the election, was quickly demolished by these hosts. They called him a Benedict Arnold repeatedly. By election time, he got barely 1 percent in a couple states.

Many conservatives listen to these shows as religiously as liberals listen to NPR – and not just during election season. They listen on the way to work, on the way home, and during the day, all throughout the year. These talk show hosts are the true thought leaders of the Republican Party. And they supported Trump unwaveringly.

Even if every single Republican elected representative had decided to oppose Trump, it would not have mattered. The talk show hosts are the kingmakers. Where they lead, conservative voters will follow.

THE FUTURE

Social media, political skepticism, and unparalleled information access is transforming the way Americans view politics. We are coming out of our sheltered childhood of accepting platitudes as reality. We have looked behind the curtain, and each day we are looking further behind the curtain.

Skepticism is high. A few decades ago, the War on Drugs was seen as necessary to protect the children. Today, it is often seen as a way to help private prisons make money. Even in the early 2000s, Bush's "They hate us for our freedom," worked. Today, any politician who tried to get away with that kind of Hallmark jingoism would be a laughingstock.

In *Lean In*, Sheryl Sandberg (COO of Facebook) argues that the division between the personal self and the professional self should disappear. She says that "I am now a true believer in bringing our whole selves to work... Instead of putting on some kind of fake 'all-work persona,' I think we benefit from expressing our truth...."

This creates a complex situation. Those whose personal lives are, "Mother hoping she can fulfill her professional ambitions while helping her children self-actualize" can probably make that happen. That mindset is safe for work. But a young man or woman who is actively hunting for sex, or unapologetically cheating, might find things a bit trickier.

In the past, bringing that type of personal life into the workplace was allowed. This was long before dirty jokes were considered sexual harassment, when most workplaces were almost entirely male.

When the world demands a single self that exists in both the professional and private world, there are two basic directions. One is a sanitized private life. The other is private degeneracy seeping into the professional world. Both are possible. Both have happened, and will happen.

The same is true in politics. When a politician's personal life was off limits, politicians had a major separation between their public persona and their private reality. That gave us John F. Kennedy, who maintained an appropriate public image despite constant womanizing.

Today, the personal life is fair game. For some people, who prefer a traditional private life, that's no big deal. For those who do not prefer that, things are a bit more complex. Eventually, they must choose to be cautious or brazen. But as information becomes more and more available, "cautious" becomes a less realistic option.

When Bill Clinton was running, he was asked if he used marijuana. He gave the phony answer, "I didn't inhale." It made him look morally degenerate, weak, and cowardly. Obama learned from that. When asked about his marijuana use, he said, "I inhaled frequently. That was the point." It made him look honest and socially intelligent.

Trump never really apologized for his history of womanizing. While he never used the words, the subtext appears to be, "Yes, as a famous billionaire I slept with many women. That was the point."

Those who vote based on personality will have a choice between unapologetic brazenness and saccharine facades of polite decency. They will have Trump's rough hewn womanizing on one side, and Hillary's inauthentic political marriage on the other.

When it comes down to it, most people will prefer a rough truth to a pretty lie.

Already, behavior that was considered the end of any career has become socially accepted. There are plenty of openly gay politicians and business leaders.

But I think the long term result will be this: people will care less and less about politicians' private lives, and more and more about their policies. We already have the ability to track and influence congressional votes in real time. Many politicians post their votes and rationale on social media, or even use social media to get input from constituents.

Personality politics may never leave completely. But as policy politics becomes more dominant, as Americans grow out of the easily-distracted-by-scandal phase and into a new phase of realism, we will see a shift in policies, not just politics.

Consider the string of voter referendums legalizing marijuana. There was no personality involved. There was just a law people wanted, and they made it happen. They overran legislatures using referendums, even when that meant open defiance of federal law.

What's next? Referendums to lower taxes? Voter pressure ending wars? People are just starting to flex their political muscles, and now they have the information they need to make big changes happen.

ADAPTING TO THE PRESENT

The 2016 election should be a wakeup call for the Democratic Party, and a warning for every other political organization. The strategic considerations brought forth by Hillary Clinton's surprising loss are as relevant to the Republican, Green, and Libertarian parties as they are to the Democrats.

Political movements must engage in active outreach to be successful. They must avoid the temptation to hide in echo chambers and safe spaces. They must recognize the difference between those who agree with them, and those who are afraid to speak their minds. Political silence should not be confused with political agreement.

Political movements should also recognize and embrace the modern voter's preference for authenticity. The era in which an extramarital affair or a dirty joke would ruin a political career has passed. Americans have grown out of that sheltered, political childhood.

Personality will always matter in politics. But the personality of "pro-status-quo ladder climber" will no longer be the gold standard. Hillary Clinton's and Mitt Romney's electoral defeats have made that clear.

Instead, politicians will have to embrace the kind of blunt authenticity that worked for both Trump and Obama. Obama's blunt admission that he "inhaled frequently – that was the point", showed real honesty. Trump's constant bluntness did the same. The era of the old, sanctimonious politician has ended.

And of course, unless polling methods change from crude snapshots to predictive models, no one should rely on them at all. In 2016 alone, these primitive methods incorrectly predicted the results of the Brexit vote and the U.S. presidential election. No financial institution, insurance company, internet advertising company, or casino would ever rely on anything so inaccurate. No one in politics should take them at all seriously.

All political parties should beware of the increase in the numbers of highly skeptical, high-information voters. These voters will not be impressed by the candidate who is the best at kissing babies or who gets the most celebrity endorsements. They will be influenced primarily by specific policy plans. Those policy plans must be clearly presented in national political messaging to attract this growing voting bloc.

Political parties should take heed of the growing number of successful voter referendums that have overturned state and federal laws. The various marijuana legalization initiatives are the obvious example. Voters have made it clear: they will have the laws they want, with or without the help of politicians. And for every voter who takes the major step of supporting a referendum, a thousand more are dissatisfied with the laws their representatives are supporting.

The 2016 Hillary Clinton loss is just one indicator of major political shifts in American politics. Living by the old standards will not work going forward. America is ready to grow politically, and politicians and the media must adapt or lose.

ABOUT THE AUTHOR

Arvin Vohra is a political strategist, social media analyst, and entrepreneur. He has been interviewed on MS-NBC, CBS, FOX, several major radio shows, and various international news shows. He is the current Vice Chair of the Libertarian National Committee.

Arvin is also the founder of Vohra Method, a private educational service specializing in online tutoring. His other books include *Lies, Damned Lies, and College Admissions* and *The Equation for Excellence.*